THE SOUTH

The Jacobin series features short interrogations of politics, economics, and culture from a socialist perspective, as an avenue to radical political practice. The books offer critical analysis and engagement with the history and ideas of the Left in an accessible format.

The series is a collaboration between Verso Books and *Jacobin* magazine, which is published quarterly in print and online at jacobinmag.com.

Other titles in this series available from Verso Books:

THE SOUTH

Jim Crow and Its Afterlives

Adolph L. Reed Jr.

With a Foreword by
Barbara J. Fields

VERSO
London • New York

To
Kenneth W. Warren and Alex W. Willingham,
who inspired this project
And
Barbara Jeanne Fields and Faith Childs,
who made sure it came to fruition

First published by Verso 2022
© Adolph L. Reed Jr. 2022
Foreword © Barbara J. Fields 2022

1 3 5 7 9 10 8 6 4 2

Verso
UK: 6 Meard Street, London W1F 0EG
US: 20 Jay Street, Suite 1010, Brooklyn, NY 11201
versobooks.com

Verso is the imprint of New Left Books

ISBN-13: 978-1-83976-626-8
ISBN-13: 978-1-83976-629-9 (US EBK)
ISBN-13: 978-1-83976-628-2 (UK EBK)

British Library Cataloguing in Publication Data
A catalogue record for this book is available from the British Library

Library of Congress Cataloging-in-Publication Data
A catalog record for this book is available from the Library of Congress

Typeset in Garamond Pro by MJ&N Gavan, Truro, Cornwall
Printed and bound by CPI Group (UK) Ltd, Croydon CR0 4YY

Contents

Foreword

by Barbara J. Fields

At a small deserted airport in El Dorado, Arkansas, during the spring of 1966, Adolph L. Reed Jr. faced a potentially life-and-death choice. Obliged unexpectedly to wait nearly three hours for a connecting flight, he approached the terminal to find two waiting room entrances, one at each end of the building. He had grown up in the Jim Crow South, so he knew what that meant. But since segregation in public accommodations had been against the law for two years, there were no signs to indicate which waiting room was which. Nor, on a Sunday afternoon (Palm Sunday or Easter Sunday, he recalls), was there a gathering of people in either one to provide a clue. Bearing vividly in mind recent high-profile murders of Northern white civil rights workers and frequent, anonymous assassinations of local black ones, Reed chose to avoid a potentially deadly mistake by waiting outdoors for his connecting flight (see pp. 46–8). Among the lessons of *The South* is that tyrannical regimes can be at their most unpredictable and treacherous in the midst of dissolution.

Reed lays out the political stakes of his account early in the introduction. Despite popular history's fixing on slavery as "the essentially formative black American experience," Reed insists that "it is Jim Crow—the regime of codified, rigorously and unambiguously enforced racism and white supremacy—that has had the most immediate consequences for contemporary life and the connections between race and politics." He makes good that insistence by knitting his recollections as a participant witness during the declining years of the Jim Crow system into an acute analysis of American politics from the mid-twentieth century to the early twenty-first.

Participants are not always the best chroniclers, let alone the best analysts, of transformations as profound as the dissolution of the Jim Crow system in the South. For persons taking daily part in such a system, the routine can so overshadow significant but subtle details that deviations from the baseline barely register as blips when they occur. After the fact, they may disappear altogether into the "Nothing has changed" or "*Plus ça change plus c'est la même chose*" aphorisms that journalists, activists, and the lay public so readily invoke when discussing post–civil rights America. Public memory of Jim Crow tends, as a result, to become a stencil. Toggling between a blurb and a melodrama, the stencil seldom affords either a rounded picture of everyday people's everyday lives or an adequate analysis of whose interests the system served, how it disintegrated, and what replaced it. The difficulty stems, in part, from what E. P. Thompson called the "condescension of posterity."[1] But the main problem is that many of those looking back—whether scholars, journalists, memoirists, or current activists—lack the analytical or imaginative wherewithal to reconcile Jim Crow as a daily lived experience with the standpoint of observers and analysts today, for whom life under Jim Crow lies beyond the threshold of memory.

Reed has the needed wherewithal, thanks to the happenstance of when he was born, the geography of his childhood, and a career spent cultivating the instincts and skills of an activist, political commentator, scholar, and teacher. First of all, as he tells readers, he belongs to the last age cohort for which the Jim Crow regime is a living memory. Furthermore, he enjoys the analytic advantages of the outside insider. Although a Southerner on both sides of his lineage and raised as an "expatriate New Orleanian," he was born in the Bronx and lived for a time in Brooklyn. As a child, he moved around within as well as beyond the "cotton curtain," attending early elementary school and making his first communion in Washington, DC, before his family moved first to Pine Bluff, Arkansas, and then to New Orleans, where his mother's family roots were. Travel within the South imposed a need for periodic refresher training in the "local option wrinkles" of Jim Crow discipline, protocols that became second nature to stay-at-home natives and whose violation, even unknowingly by a child, could bring a death sentence—as it did for fourteen-year-old Emmet Till in 1955. Because learning the rules of Jim Crow could not be a one-and-done matter for him, Reed never achieved that degree of taking-for-granted that could render the details opaque to his own subsequent analysis.

Jim Crow was a series of locally varying accents within which the basic language was clear. "Ef it wuzn't fer them polices 'n' them ol' lynch-mobs," a friend of Richard Wright's remarked sardonically, "there wouldn't be nothin' but uproar down here!"[2] "Nothin' but uproar" may have been intentional hyperbole since, even under a barbaric regime such as Jim

Crow, people cannot live constantly at fever pitch. More likely, Wright's friend thought "uproar" an apt characterization of an everyday routine that, even when uneventful, unfolded amid tyrannical restrictions and an ever-looming threat of capricious violence.

With the eyes, ears, and keen political antennae of the outside insider, Reed picks out the quotidian routine within the uproar, bringing the quotidian to light without minimizing or losing sight of the uproar. The result is an uncommon tour of the Jim Crow world of his childhood and young adulthood, revealing, as he moves from place to place, a diversity of rules, textures, and colors that contradict the stencil version. For one thing, the rigid residential segregation of Southern cities that grew up after the Civil War did not prevail in Old South cities such as New Orleans. Reed offers a fascinating account of the ways black and white neighbors in New Orleans did and did not deal with each other, with some acknowledgments of each other permissible within the neighborhood but forbidden outside it. "News that eggplants, satsumas, Creole tomatoes, crawfish, or mirlitons had appeared in markets, announcing their seasons' arrival, was much too vital information to be blocked by the color line," he reports, for example (pp. 18–19). He also recounts the rules that his family learned, perforce, as part of daily life: which shops allowed black customers to try on hats but not shoes, which shoes but not hats, which forbade them to try on anything, and which imposed conditions so demeaning that his family refused to patronize them at all. And then there was a McCrory's Five and Dime whose strawberry ice cream sodas were so good that, as a child, he barely registered the Jim Crow window he had to patronize in order to enjoy them (p. 98). Once, during a crossing on the segregated Algiers Ferry, his grandmother explained why they had to sit behind a chicken-wire barrier, her voice clearly pitched for the white people on the other side of the barrier to hear: "Well, you see, a lot of crazy people ride this ferry, and they have to sit on the other side" (p. 12).

By design, the Jim Crow system overrode class distinctions among Afro-Americans, subjecting all, at least notionally, to the leveling discipline of white supremacy. Even so, middle-class black professionals and businesspeople, Reed reports, "were better able than others to shield themselves from both the everyday indignities and the atrocities of the Jim Crow world" (p. 41). They were less apt to be under the daily supervision of white superiors and could minimize (though not completely eliminate) social contacts that might require demeaning acts of subservience. Those circumstances account for the prominence of the black middle class in the leadership of the civil rights movement. At the same time, as Reed illustrates in an account of the 1970s Soul City project in North Carolina (pp. 82–6), taking them into account refutes any assumption that the black-white binary and accompanying class dynamics could have persisted unchanged from the Jim Crow era into the post–civil rights movement era.

In analyzing the phenomenon of "passing" for white—*passant blanc*, as it was known in New Orleans—Reed subjects the current preoccupation with "identity" and "authenticity" to a salutary cold-water bath. Whether at the level of a group or that of an individual, he argues, passing tended to be instrumental rather than existential and had little or nothing to do with identity. "In a rigidly hierarchical social order based on ascriptive status," he reminds readers, "the inclination to differentiate oneself from groups consigned to the bottom, while not laudable, is reasonable and understandable" (p. 75). The tragi-comic saga of the Haliwa of North Carolina serves as a case in point. After persuading the state legislature to change their birth certificate designation from "colored" to "Indian" and, eventually, to ratify a segregated school system for their newly established group, they had no time to enjoy their victory before school desegregation and civil rights laws rendered it meaningless. In the thick of their campaign to carve out an exemption for themselves from the strictures of the Jim Crow system, they did not recognize that the system itself stood on the verge of collapse (pp. 73–4, 87–8).

Reed's own family turned passing to instrumental effect by occasionally begging his grandmother and her daughter—the only two members whose appearance made it practicable—to enter a white-only establishment in order to buy particularly delicious beignets, the signature doughnuts of New Orleans. In doing so, he reports, neither woman "experienced any existential anxiety, not even a speed bump" or "considered for an instant that perpetrating that deception reflected at all on herself, her values or identity" (p. 99).

The possibility of sudden, deadly violence remained latent in the everyday as the Jim Crow system tottered on its last legs. (Nor is it absent today, as Trayvon Martin and others learned in their last moments.) At the same time, ambiguity so permeated some situations that only the ultimate outcome could reveal when danger was real. Reed recounts two notable occasions when what might have been fraught encounters turned out to be innocuous. The first occurred while Reed was driving from Atlanta to New Orleans with his then four-year-old son, Touré, and was stranded at night on a deserted roadside in Alabama by a faulty alternator. A white sheriff's deputy appeared and drove them to a motel in a nearby town, pointing out the shop of a mechanic who could tow and perhaps repair the car in the morning. The punchline comes when Reed and his son are alone in the motel and Touré (now a distinguished scholar in his own right) remarks to his father: "Daddy, I almost told him to get out of the black community, but I thought I shouldn't" (pp. 66). As can happen when young children are learning to imitate adult conversation, Touré had picked up the vocabulary and perhaps the grammar of movement activism but had not yet mastered the syntax.

The second occasion occurred during the mid-1970s. Reed and his family were driving on an interstate highway near Greenville, South Carolina, when a state trooper followed and finally stopped their car. Summoned to the trooper's car, where he found himself "staring into the barrel of a shotgun affixed under the glove box," Reed discovered that the trooper had simply been baffled by his "Boycott Gulf" bumper sticker. Rather than facing intimidation or worse, he ended up satisfying the trooper's curiosity by delivering an impromptu tutorial about Portuguese colonialism in Africa (pp. 60–1).

Running through *The South* is an analysis directed as much at understanding today's politics as the politics that underpinned the Jim Crow system. For example, Reed offers a sustained explication—sometimes implicit, sometimes explicit—of why "white supremacy," is useless as a tool of analysis, however potent it may be as a slogan. During the heyday of Jim Crow, "white supremacy" as a political slogan successfully camouflaged differences of class purpose and standpoint among its white constituencies. "States' rights" performed a similar service in the pre–Civil War South—until Confederate war measures that fell unequally on different classes of white people burned away the veneer. The re-enfranchisement of black voters similarly burned away the veneer as Jim Crow disintegrated. Some of the most arresting sections of *The South* analyze the ensuing redesign and redeployment of class power—among Afro-Americans as well as in American society as a whole.

Soi-disant progressives are more likely these days to invoke "white supremacy" than are troglodyte racists. Together with the habit of according slavery pride of place as "the essentially formative black American experience," the vogue of "white supremacy" as both political analysis and organizing slogan lends urgency to one of Reed's key warnings: that mistaking familiar imagery for actual continuity (for example, by identifying voting restrictions or the disproportionate incarceration of black persons as a new Jim Crow) "obscure[s] how the present differs most meaningfully from the past" (p. 111). Failure to grasp the differences condemns persons of good will to fight the last war while letting the present one go by default. In setting aside the stencil version of the Jim Crow past, Reed challenges the stencil version of current politics, mapping the terrain on which a constructive politics can take shape.

Through decades as a political activist, journalist, scholar, and teacher, Adolph Reed has consistently advocated a serious, historically grounded, and genuinely progressive politics. Attentive readers of the following pages will learn how he arrived at his understanding of the past, his analysis of the present, his diagnosis of where politics has gone astray, and his prescription for where it needs to go from here. They may well, as a result, be inspired to think anew about the prospects for building a more humane world—and the steps, in thought and in action, that will be required to bring it about.

Introduction

In the early years of this century, on sporadic visits to the South after having left the region completely during Ronald Reagan's first months in the White House, I was constantly struck by how much the ways that things had changed in the region seemed to underscore the ways they hadn't, and, vice versa, how the ways things haven't changed underscore the ways they have. Going there was like traveling back in time, yet at the same time not.

I had this reaction in the more cosmopolitan big cities like New Orleans and Atlanta as well as in the smaller cities that have grown and morphed since the defeat of the Jim Crow social order, like the Research Triangle in North Carolina and Richmond and the Hampton-Newport News area of Virginia. It was maybe even more striking in mid-sized, older cities with Deep South histories, like Charleston, South Carolina; Jackson, Mississippi; Shreveport, Louisiana; or Little Rock, Arkansas. Continuity and change seem most indistinguishably linked, mutually signifying, in the smaller, less bustling cities and towns—like Bamberg and Spartanburg in South Carolina; Fayetteville and Rocky Mount, North Carolina; Columbus and Albany, Georgia; Tallulah and Ferriday, Louisiana; Lake Village and Dumas, Arkansas; Greenville and Meridian, Mississippi; and the legendary Selma and Eutaw, Alabama— where local elites had not been leavened so much by infusions from outside.

When I tried to communicate my reaction to others, I usually feared that I seemed to be just babbling. As I say it, it sounds like the old cliché, "the more things change, the more they stay the same," with an inflection of New Age-y circularity. I suspect that most people to whom I've made the observation nod politely while finding my description utterly meaningless. But a few, mainly those with personal experience of the Jim Crow regime of the segregation era, have understood intuitively the sense I tried to convey. This isn't surprising; that regime, which lasted for roughly the first two-thirds of the twentieth century, was the region's social, political, economic, and ideological cornerstone, the source of its most important identity and institutions.

I think my reaction was so viscerally unsettling and my description so inadequate partly for the same reasons. So much of what the old order was, what it depended on for the sense of naturalness that any social order requires to seem stable and legitimate, was tacit and mundane. The architecture of laws and prohibitions—the state constitutional and legislative mandate of white supremacy under the bogus principle of "separate but equal" and all its local-option wrinkles of enforcement—was the brute reality that defined the boundaries of everyday life, set the limits of aspiration. It was the foundation on which developed the unspoken rules and codes that most immediately governed everyone's behavior, beliefs, life chances, and views of others. This is indeed one of the smaller ironies of the current attention to recuperating slavery as the essentially formative black American experience; it is Jim Crow—the regime of codified, rigorously, and unambiguously enforced racism and white supremacy—that has had the most immediate consequences for contemporary life and the connections between race and politics in the South and, less directly, the rest of the country.

Ongoing renegotiation of the relation between race and power and opportunity, or what is more delicately called "race relations," lies at the heart of this sensation of the eerie connection of past and present, which, I should point out, is the experience of a familiar outsider, an expatriate. It's normal life for those—black, white, and other—whose daily actions and calculations make the region's evolving accommodations to the key victories of the civil rights movement: the 1964 Civil Rights law that overturned official segregation and, perhaps more important in the long term, the 1965 Voting Rights law, twice since amended and renewed, that has meant that black people could no longer be so easily castigated and suppressed or their interests so flagrantly ignored in politics and public policy. It was, after all, elimination of blacks from the electorate that made the Jim Crow regime possible in the first place. But that's a story to which I'll return.

One needn't have experienced the old order firsthand to know it and therefore to recognize its persistence and passage in today's South. But having lived through it can give a special sensitivity to its nuances and to the ways in which it was encoded in people's everyday lives. This can be a self-serving view, but I believe that level of awareness is more common among those of us who experienced the segregationist regime as subordinates, as those who were, in the idiom of the time,

Jim Crowed. Others could live it blithely, which is not to say that all of them always did. But we couldn't afford to. Passing conversations years later with white contemporaries have revealed both the radically different social maps we operated with in the same places at the same times and how easy it could be for them, especially as kids, to live obliviously even through the paroxysms of the regime's death agonies in the 1960s.

In most of their daily affairs most of the time people normally aren't focused on the architecture of the social system that gives direction to and shapes the content of their lives, their dreams and fears, their sense of who they are and what they deserve—just as we don't think about the architecture of the buildings we inhabit or pass by and through, unless we feel them shaking or foundering around us. Otherwise, we live and daily reproduce our social systems subtly, in small, apparently superficial acts. And the Jim Crow system, once consolidated, was by and large lived that way, in little rituals of deference and superiority, in gestures and accommodations that assumed, and thereby reinforced, the walls, floors, ceilings, and foundation of white supremacy.

This leads to another reason that my summary description of the South today may not resonate for most others. I was eighteen when President Lyndon Johnson signed the Voting Rights Act into law, not quite nine when the Montgomery bus boycott crystallized the aggressive protest phase of the civil rights movement, ten when Little Rock exploded over the desegregation of Central High. (Today a huge image of the school greets arrivals to the municipal airport.) Only the most precocious of southerners even ten years my junior have conscious recollections of the social system they were living in and its textures. My age cohort is basically the last, black or white, for which the Jim Crow regime is a living memory—for good and ill. Even though we largely grew up together, my closest cousins, a decade or so younger than I, came to consciousness in a New Orleans in which official segregation was no longer a reality with rules they had to master, on pain of possible life or death consequences.

Probably most of us who reached adulthood under that system's heel have been indelibly marked by it. I know that, even at my advanced age, I can flare into blind rage when confronted with a white person's assertion of peremptory, arbitrary authority over me, and I become almost equally incensed by what I interpret as their expressions of presumptuous racial entitlement and prerogative. As national politics moved ever more rightward in the 1980s and 1990s, my oldest friend (who is from Shreveport, Louisiana and has lived for more than three decades in New England) and I would joke occasionally that we felt sorry for our sons, about the same age, because, when Jim Crow returned, they wouldn't know how to act properly. The obvious implication is that we've never forgotten how. Indeed, now and again, as the business class car on Amtrak fills up, I flash on Homer Adolph Plessy's attempted 1892 trip from New Orleans to nearby Covington—the first step in the *Plessy v. Ferguson* case in which the US Supreme Court in 1896 established the notorious "separate but equal" doctrine that legitimized Jim Crow—and imagine the conductor ordering me to give up my seat for a white passenger.

But that's only scar tissue. There's no chance that that regime will return, at least not on terms familiar to its survivors. Yet there are other reasons that perspectives of the diminishing ranks of those who experienced Jim Crow on a daily basis could be worthwhile.

The everyday life of the segregation era is not much discussed
outside the world of academic specialists. More attention is
given to large events—court decisions, laws, protest campaigns
—and to the heroism of the movement; the horror of extraor-
dinary racist militants like Bull Connor, the notorious Public
Safety Commissioner of Birmingham, and Byron de la Beck-
with, the Klansman who murdered Medgar Evers; and large
outrages like lynchings, bombings, and murders of civil rights
activists. Missing from these discussions is a sense of how the
segregationist regime was held together, what practical purposes it served and for whom, what it ultimately *was*. It is
identified with abstractions like prejudice, bigotry, racism,
and most recently an eternal White Supremacy, which tell us
nothing about how the order operated, how its official and
unofficial protocols organized people's lives.

Those without intimate knowledge of the regime are left
with a vague sense of it as the bad old days when bigots and
bigotry reigned. That impression obscures the most basic truth
of the white supremacist South: it was a coherent social order,
constructed and maintained by specific social interests through
political and economic institutions that channeled the experience of everyone in the region. Even the familiar imagery
of separate water fountains, lunch counters, and restrooms
feeds misunderstanding by representing those features as the
summary reality of segregation. Although its intent is usually
the exact opposite, this picture of the Jim Crow era reduces
segregation to its most superficial artifacts, like reducing the
image of an iceberg to its visible tip.

It also encourages two apparently opposite misunderstand-
ings. On the one hand is a view that simplistically celebrates
defeat of the segregationist regime as also the defeat of

entrenched inequality, which is a species of the same genus as contentions that Barack Obama's election to the presidency demonstrated that the country had become "postracial." On the other hand, a view expressed more and more commonly as the era recedes in time contends that the civil rights movement's victories were trivial. An extension of this view, which was retailed by Malcolm X and other black race nationalists, is that the struggle against segregation was misdirected, that fighting to desegregate lunch counters and restrooms, for example, reflected a demeaning presumption that black people needed proximity to whites for their validation. The problem, we hear with disturbing frequency and emphatic self-confidence, particularly from younger people, was not the principle of "separate but equal" but the fact that it wasn't honestly enforced. These contentions fundamentally misunderstand the reality of the Jim Crow order.

Separate never was intended to be equal. The sole purpose of the segregationist regime, which did not take shape until the 1890s and early 1900s, was to enforce racial inequality and black subordination, as a virtue on its own and as an instrument of other ends. As legal historian Charles A. Lofgren shows in *The Plessy Case: A Legal-Historical Interpretation,* until that time mandatory racial separation in various areas of social life was episodic, almost random.[1] In the decades after the Civil War (or, more precisely, the Treasonous Insurrection of the Slaveholding Elites of Eleven States against the Constitutional Government of the United States), states and localities imposed racial regulations on public transportation, education, and other areas and rescinded them, or initially didn't regulate racial contact and later imposed separation and in some cases later overturned the mandated separation.

Segregation, Lofgren argues, was not a major focal point for southern or black politics until it became an element of reassertion of planter and merchant class power after the defeat of Reconstruction and the Populist insurgency at the end of the nineteenth century. As a systematic social order, its purpose was to impose through law and social regulation a doctrine of white supremacy that established boundaries on the politically thinkable in much the same way that anti-communism would nationally during the post–World War II decades. It is worthy of note as well that the victorious ruling class didn't impose the regime in most places until blacks (and many poor or working-class whites) had been taken out of the political equation by disfranchising them.

The relatively superficial mechanisms that were elements of enforcement—the petty apartheid of Jim Crow take-out windows at restaurants, separate water fountains, toilets, and so on—were never trivial to those who endured them on a daily basis and were never less than massively inconvenient and humiliating. And everyone understood that they were extrusions inseparably linked—as the tip is to the submerged 90 percent of an iceberg—to that larger system that included denial of due process and equal protection under the law and the extremes of economic exploitation made possible by elimination of citizenship rights. "Separate but equal" was first, last, and always no more than a paper-thin ruse to support the fiction that this system did not violate black people's constitutional protections as citizens.

The superficial view of the Jim Crow world has contributed to spreading a confused understanding of black southerners' accommodation, compensation, and resistance to segregation. It also makes it harder to make sense of the contemporary

South and to recognize its contradictions and possibilities. Perhaps reflecting on how people actually lived it can help to address some of that confusion. If not, then I hope at least to record facets and textures that might otherwise be lost as the era passes from living memory.

My rootedness in the South always had a small asterisk. My parents were both natives: my mother a New Orleanian, my father from the Arkansas Delta region, though he left for Chicago as a young man. Most of my grandparents were born hardly more than a generation away from plantation slavery in the United States. My paternal grandfather was born in southeast Arkansas in 1875, my grandmother a decade or so later, from an Exoduster family who moved from Alabama to Arkansas in pursuit of opportunity. The Reeds hail from a couple of defunct hamlets in Desha County called Reed and Reedville, both settled by former slaves owned by a planter of the same name. (I've often quipped that Grambling College and New York Knicks' basketball legend Willis Reed, from just across the state line in northeast Louisiana, and bluesman Jimmy Reed, from the other side of the river in Mississippi, and my family are probably all related by prior condition of ownership, possibly with ancestors who showed up on the same bill of sale.) My maternal grandmother began her century on the planet in 1897 in Pointe Coupee Parish, Louisiana, though all her immediate family relocated to Tampico, Mexico and a couple of generations later to San Antonio, Texas. My mother's father was a Cuban immigrant, from Oriente, born in 1894. So we've pretty well covered the Gulf of Mexico, more thoroughly with the Miami/South Florida contingent that arrived between the 1960s and the 2000s. All my American grandparents were living links, through their own parents and grandparents, to slavery and Reconstruction. On my father's side, mainly in his generation, we've been part of the big demographic movement that contributed to the blackening of the Midwest—St. Louis (the de facto capital of Arkansas), Chicago, Indianapolis, Kankakee (Illinois).

My parents were part of the movement out of the South as well. So I was born in the Bronx, lived for a time in Brooklyn, and did my early grammar school years in Washington, DC. I made my First Communion at a racially integrated Catholic school and parish in Washington in 1954, the day before the US Supreme Court, a five-minute walk away, handed down the decision in *Brown v. Topeka Board of Education* that overturned *Plessy* and outlawed official segregation in public education.

New Orleanians often live in the rest of the United States somewhat like immigrants—shipping, transporting, and yearning for quantities of local delicacies and oddities—and relatives at "home" tend to treat those living elsewhere as if they've gone to some foreign land, even if it's as nearby as Dallas or Birmingham. This phenomenon has continued with the population dispersal after the cataclysm of Hurricane Katrina. Partly for that reason, I was raised somewhat as an expatriate New Orleanian. I was as often as not there on vacations and for summers, with trips occasionally timed to see the family barber. As these visits in the early years originated from places beyond the Cotton Curtain, I had to have segregation's everyday boundaries explained to me repeatedly—separate lines, "buzzard roost" balconies in those segregated movie theaters we could enter at all, separate seating on the Mississippi River ferry and in buses and streetcars, customarily segregated

Communion lines at Mass in "white" parishes. Some stores and restaurants we couldn't enter. In some department stores we could try on hats but not shoes; in others the rules were reversed. There were Jim Crow restrooms, water fountains and waiting rooms in all public buildings as well as most white doctors' offices and hospitals, benches that could be sat on here but not there. The Audubon Zoo pony ride was off-limits, as was the "public" pool in City Park, the amusement park, and most of the recreational lakefront of Lake Pontchartrain.

When my cousin from New Jersey and I were visiting during the summer we were both six years old, our grandmother took us to the zoo, and on spying the pony ride, we instantly became excited about riding. The ride's operator pointed out that we were forbidden from riding. I can't recall his demeanor in denying us. I do know that my cousin Gwendolyn and I cried and that my grandmother dressed him down rather severely for being heartless and small-minded, to no avail. For his part, I presume that, no matter how committed he may or may not have been to Jim Crow personally, he may simply not have wanted to jeopardize his job by breaking the law or convention. Another incident involving learning the codes had a less fraught conclusion. As a small child, I loved taking rides back and forth across the river on the Algiers Ferry; perhaps that helped prepare for the circumstance that my main high school girlfriend lived on the West Bank (which at that point in the river's course actually lies east of most of New Orleans). On one trip, I noticed that on the main passenger level, the deck was bifurcated by chicken wire with some passengers sitting on one side of the wire and others on the other, and I asked my grandmother why that was. We were sitting on a bench right next to the separating wire, and she said in a stage whisper, "Well, you see, a lot of crazy people ride this ferry, and they have to sit on the other side."

Even after my parents and I moved into the South, the special instructions were still necessary; every city or town enforced "separate but equal" in slightly different ways. Black people were always expected to know the local rules and etiquette; mistakes, including those made in complete ignorance, could be deadly, and age was no excuse. Fourteen-year-old Emmett Till was murdered in nearby Mississippi on a family visit from Chicago in 1955 because he unknowingly violated a local rule of racial subordination in a way that was interpreted as "getting fresh" with a white woman. But, as a small child, I couldn't grasp the big picture or the nature of the dangers or the reasons for the restrictions and what they added up to.

We moved to Pine Bluff, Arkansas, where my father took his first professorial position at the black state college, a year or so before the eruption in Little Rock, forty miles away. For most of the next quarter-century I lived mainly in the South— there, New Orleans, where I spent my high school years, North Carolina, and Atlanta. I left the region during Ronald Reagan's first year in the White House and have returned only on visits, though fairly frequent ones.

I always felt like only partly a southerner, though I lived there through the entire duration of the activist phase of the civil rights movement, the decomposition and collapse of the Jim Crow order, and the formation of the new political and social regime that would replace it. I even worked for several years in the administration of Atlanta's first black mayor, Maynard Jackson. Nonetheless, moving to the Northeast felt like another version of going back home, after a long absence; the scents of the New York subway system and roasting chestnuts had never left me or lost their association with the earliest childhood feelings of warmth and security, and the regional topography never stopped feeling like the natural environment. I confess also that I'm still deeply affected by the moving inscriptions on Grand Army of the Republic veterans' tombstones in old New England cemeteries. No doubt this emotion has been charged by half a life of unmitigated, never abating outrage at the pandemic, relentless, matter-of-fact celebration of the Confederacy I endured in its former domain, along with its equally matter-of-fact and ubiquitous Big Lie about Emancipation and Reconstruction. Small wonder that the only scene in *Gone with the Wind* (which I refused to watch a minute of until I was in my thirties) I've ever been able to stomach is the burning of Atlanta.

Nevertheless, I am also a southerner—and a New Orleanian, as a friend pointed out when, during a visit to Little Rock several years ago, I made a passing reference to having been "up in Shreveport" not too long before. I know the South as an insider, but at the same time as enough of an outsider—a status reinforced by having lived in different places in and parts of the region, and therefore always having to think through the idiosyncrasies of segregation's local codes—that the regime was never fully second nature to me. I don't pretend to having had a sensitivity to oppression that my peers and others lacked. If bristling at Jim Crow's injustices was especially prominent in my consciousness, it was partly because, as a result of moving around, I was always struggling to learn the local rules and grammar of subordination and how to craft a normal kid's and adolescent's life within them. Where I lived and my family's class position also made it easier to cultivate and express indignation.

All four of my grandparents had attended college. My father's parents were what used to be called "educators." One of his cousins, a teacher in Little Rock, was plaintiff in the 1940s lawsuit that won equalization of pay for black and white public schoolteachers. Such suits were brought in many southern states, and their success was one element in the segregationist order's dismantlement. My family in New Orleans lived mainly within Catholic middle-class circles, as insulated as it was possible to be from arbitrary white racial power. When I started high school, my grandfather insisted that I carry business cards from a half-dozen or so police captains and lieutenants he counted as friends. One I recall was a mounted cop at the Fair Grounds racetrack who some years earlier had hoisted me up for my only experience being on a horse. Another was the father of Cleveland Indians shortstop George Strickland. The elder Strickland and my grandfather were so close that, when the Indians went to the 1954 World Series, he gave my grandfather, who was a huge baseball fan, tickets to the games in Cleveland. He was delighted and loved the experience; my father and I rooted for the Giants and were therefore happier with the Series outcome.

1

Quotidian Life in the 1950s and 1960s

The regime was less harsh in New Orleans in some respects than in other big cities in the region. In some ways it's never been a typically southern city. Even the local speech isn't typically southern. When I moved to North Carolina to go to college, I had to train my ear to hear properly what we usually think of as southern accents and to make class and regional distinctions among them. Within a few years after leaving the South in the early 1980s, I found that my ability to hear those accents naturally, without straining to understand, had dissipated; for a while, on trips back I had to pause and translate communications in my head, as one does with a seldom-used second language.

On the one hand, the local political culture in New Orleans managed, and still does, to combine features of conventional southern and Latin or Caribbean Catholic conservatism. On the other hand, the Big Easy and the City That Care Forgot monikers, though primarily tourist industry hype, reflected something genuine—a laid-back local style that could wink more easily than most at petty, private transgressions, so long as they were conducted unobtrusively or, as Cubans today describe the gap between official policy and unofficially recognized practice there, *bajo la mesa* (under the table). No doubt many facts nudged in that direction: the port; the diversity of immigrant populations, often with their own living histories of discrimination (as, for instance, the group of eleven Sicilians lynched in the city in 1891 for allegedly assassinating the police chief or the tens of thousands of Irish canal diggers who died and were buried in the New Basin Canal in the 1830s); and the democratizing realities of Mafia-led wide-openness. (Prideful local lore has it that the Black Hand extortion arrived in the city from Sicily before it showed up in New York.) And the city's quirks of housing occupancy, which stemmed from its age and length of settlement, may also have had some effect.

In much of the city, the pattern of residential segregation was more like a checkerboard than racial separation on strict geographical lines. Blacks and whites frequently lived in the same neighborhoods, on different sides of the street or different ends of the block. There was not normally a lot of interaction across racial lines; sharing recipes and popping over for neighborly cups of coffee were rare occurrences at best. Black and white residents didn't so much share neighborhoods as coexist in them. They presumably had their neighborhood life, and we had ours—all in the same space. Some whites obviously recoiled at having black neighbors and went out of their way to underscore the barriers between them and us. Some were aggressively hostile and passed that disposition on to their dogs and children. Many were content to live peacefully, if not amicably, within minimal standards of racial distance that were generally faithful to the norms of segregation but tacitly improvised by blacks and whites mutually—for example, no expectations of entering each other's homes, no joint social activities or excursions out of the neighborhood.

Many of those white people who were cordial in the neighborhood's everyday confines would snub or feign not to recognize their black neighbors when encountering them elsewhere. To some extent, we accurately and justifiably understood that behavior as two-faced, particularly when it came from those who seemed to display greater than usual warmth and fellow-feeling within the neighborhood's cloister. In retrospect, though, most white people were also confronted with the challenge of devising appropriate ways of being within a social order they didn't create and that came to them as the world's unquestioned and unquestionable facts of life. And the repercussions of being defined as a "nigger-lover" threatened to be almost as great as being defined as black. These could go beyond social ostracism and scorn; they could affect employment and other aspects of material well-being. People should be commended and appreciated when they are prepared to face such risks for decency or principle; it's not necessarily damnable when they aren't, though this insight comes much more easily decades after the fact. And I've gone unrecognized frequently enough—both in the South and elsewhere—by familiar white colleagues and coworkers in public situations outside our shared normal contexts that I've realized that many white people's social perception has been trained not to distinguish us as individuals within their environment. It's not so much that we "all look alike" to them, as the cliché goes. Many white people simply and genuinely do not see us distinctly unless they have specific, clearly defined expectations of doing so. Thus, Sidney Poitier, Danny Glover, and Chadwick Boseman each has been cast to play Thurgood Marshall in films though none of them bears even the most fleeting physical resemblance to him. By contrast, think of the efforts taken to cast actors who resemble, or can be made up to resemble, white historical figures like Lincoln, Winston Churchill, Richard Nixon, Roger Ailes, Hitler, or even Babe Ruth.

Those neighborhoods were by no means idyllic settings of racial harmony. They were clearly segregated. Within those limitations, however, in little ways the fact of cohabiting the same daily terrain subverted racial distance and, to that extent also the Jim Crow regime, if only at its margins. Men now and again would be drawn across the color line to kibitz or join in some spontaneously collaborative project like working on a car. Sometimes they would cross the line, at least for an inning or two, to join the small congregations that formed on porches, front yards, and sidewalks to listen to and comment on radio broadcasts of baseball games. These were first the St. Louis Cardinals, and then the Houston Astros, née Colt 45s, who had the supplanting virtues of closer proximity and featuring hometown hero, Rusty Staub, in the lineup. Occasional conversations, often only exchanges of patter, across backyards, from porches and stoops or in pedestrian encounters, about mutual, if superficial, concerns—the heat of the day, whether enough rain would come to counter the sun's scorching of plants and yards, the approach of a hurricane in the Gulf of Mexico, the behavior of rambunctious neighborhood kids, how gardens progressed and the quality of the fruit on backyard trees, prices and offerings at the corner stores, whose pipes had burst in an uncommon freeze—established moments of recognition of equivalent humanity, commonality, and connection as individuals. News that eggplants, satsumas, Creole tomatoes, crawfish, or mirlitons had appeared in markets, announcing their seasons' arrival, was information much too vital to be blocked by the color line.

Catholicism similarly could be a mild solvent in that very Catholic city, particularly at the level of the neighborhood parish. Catholic schools were racially segregated until 1962, when they were desegregated at all levels at once without major incident. This occurred two years after the public schools implemented a phased desegregation plan that provoked a months-long white uprising more generalized and at least as vicious as Little Rock had experienced in a narrower compass three years previously. The Church was hardly a beacon of racial equality and justice. However, despite the Archdiocese's accommodation and embrace of segregation, including the insane indignity of separate seating at Mass and distribution of Communion practiced in white parishes through the 1950s (though, curiously, confessional lines weren't segregated), at least on going to and coming from, entering and exiting, the parish church, black and white neighbors who were co-parishioners encountered each other on a more public plane that remained anchored to the neighborhood. The parish's organic links to the neighborhood elicited passing exchange of convivialities that could affirm in a public setting acknowledgments of equal humanity enacted more privately on the block, but could do so without the higher stakes associated with recognition in settings entirely divorced from the neighborhood. This effect was certainly marginal. Even those little encounters were too public for many whites to feel comfortably convivial. And interracial attendance at Mass wasn't the norm. Most black Catholics usually attended churches linked to the segregated black parochial schools. (In high school, my friends and I became connoisseurs of the norms of different parishes, as we shopped around among the smorgasbord of Sunday Mass offerings, sometimes seeking the latest, or the briefest, or the most conveniently located in relation to whatever other plans we had.)

These features of local everyday life and the city's size and its extent of commercial and industrial development increased the likelihood of black/white encounters that spontaneously took the shape of normal human interactions. This likelihood was greater when those encounters were outside the spotlight of public scrutiny, and it was diminished in moments of politically supercharged white supremacist fervor. Even then, though, it did not disappear entirely. A couple of instances from my own experience may illustrate this kind of encounter and its possible, if limited, significance.

When I was in the ninth grade, in either late 1959 or early 1960, a couple of friends and I often walked about seven blocks from our school on Magazine Street in the city's Uptown section to ride the St. Charles streetcar at least part of the way home. We took this route, even though the bus that stopped in front of the school was more convenient and arguably more direct, partly to dawdle and hang out and partly because both the walk and the streetcar ride were visually pleasant and serene. On the walk we had fallen into the practice of stopping at a little mom-and-pop store on Soniat Street to buy bits of the junk kids buy after school. Before long, we began to test our mettle at shoplifting. On my first or second attempt I was caught boosting a bag of potato chips or some such. The proprietors, a white couple (as I look back on it, they were probably in their late thirties), nabbed me and wouldn't let me leave with my friends. I was terrified. By that time, I knew enough about the Jim Crow world to imagine, first, the horror of the police and then being sent to Angola, the state penitentiary, or at least the juvenile reformatory—the "training school" in Baker, near Baton Rouge. Both facilities, especially Angola, were routinely held over our heads by family and other adults as the terminal destination toward which bad behavior would take us. That warning applied to violations of parental rules as well as to more public transgressions that could lead to contact with the Jim Crow criminal justice system. Even now, when I hear the word Angola, or even see it on this page, I can feel a small, internal shudder.

To my grateful surprise and tremendous relief, the couple sat me down on the store's stoop and talked to me, more like concerned parents or relatives than as intimidating or hostile storekeepers. They said that I seemed like a good kid, that they weren't going to call the police or my parents, but that I should take a lesson from this incident and not try anything like it again. They explained that I might not be so fortunate next time as to be caught by people as decent and understanding as they were and that, as a result, I could end up in a lot of trouble and maybe ruin my life. They elicited assurances that I'd seen my error and wouldn't repeat it. Then they let me leave. In effect, they treated me without hesitation as I suspect they'd have hoped for a child of their own to be treated in a similar position, notwithstanding the prevailing white suprem-acist codes that would dictate otherwise. I have no clue how they might have responded to the school desegregation crisis that hit the city the next school year or any other public issue bearing on racial equality. I know what would make for an uplifting story, but I have no illusions. All I know is that, if they had acted that afternoon in accord with the dictates of the Jim Crow social order and not seen me as they did, I could have, even with the relative insulation of class position, wound up at Baker.

The second incident occurred the previous summer and also involves a mom-and-pop store family. My neighborhood was in a section of the Hollygrove area, nestled between the Airline Highway and what had been a section of New Basin Canal, which was then drained and filled with the clam, mussel, and oyster shells that qualified as gravel in New Orleans. Shortly before I began high school, it was paved over to become the Pontchartrain Expressway and eventually part of Interstate 10. The triangular neighborhood's third boundary was the New Orleans Country Club, where many of the adult black male residents worked for some period as golf caddies, including our next-door neighbor who worked there all his life. That was where our section of Hollygrove's most distinguished product, the legendary local vocalist, Johnny Adams, developed his life-long love for the game. Other men worked as longshoremen or merchant seamen; some worked as porters, laborers, or in more skilled jobs in the building trades—plasterers, paint-ers, bricklayers—and a few worked at the Kaiser aluminum plant or other factories. There was a smattering of Protestant ministers, including Johnny's father, a couple of physicians, a few small business proprietors, and a complement of public schoolteachers, including several women. Most of the women who worked, however, were domestics. It's instructive that I never had any notion what any of the white Hollygrove resi-dents did for a living—except, that is, for the Gagliano family.

Two corner stores, a block apart, mainly served my imme-diate slice of Hollygrove, Tony's and Oddo's. "Mr. Tony" Gagliano and his family lived in the long, shotgun structure that housed their store, which was a half-block away from my house, at the intersection of my street, Pear, and Gen. Ogden. Oddo, whose store was a block farther away on Gen. Ogden, lived in the Metairie suburb, though he also may at one time have lived above his store. For years I wondered who this Gen. Ogden was and what he had done to warrant naming a street after him. I was bemused to learn decades later that he had been commander of the supremacist Crescent City White League's murderous 1874 insurrection against the Reconstruction government and its interracial Metropolitan Police. This "Battle of Liberty Place" was commemorated with a monument erected at the foot of Canal Street in 1891 and that immediately became a rallying point for the lynchers of the eleven hapless Sicilians and for many other racist initiatives spawned in the city thereafter.

The Gaglianos were generally regarded as decent and fair, though most black patrons maintained the cautious skepticism that would mediate any commercial relationship in an environment in which legal recourse couldn't be assumed even as a deterrent. "Mr. Tony"—the appellation was mutual; my grandparents were Mr. and Mrs. Mac to them—and his wife seemed almost always to chat freely and unguardedly with adult patrons, white and black, sharing neighborhood gossip, making solicitous inquiries about health and family plans and the like, and comparing notes on their own daily and family concerns. Usually they, especially Mrs. Gagliano, would ask kids about school, vacations, and such matters, and, if the kids were alone and their parents or guardians hadn't been in the store recently, inquire after them and send greetings back with the youngsters. Though Mr. Gagliano in particular could seem rather gruff on occasion, as a rule they presented themselves in a fashion best described as cordial to friendly and, well, neighborly.

Oddo's reputation was a different kettle of fish. Neither he nor his wife was cordial, and they were frequently characterized as dishonest and "mean," if not "prejudiced." Several families wouldn't send children to his store alone for fear of his shortchanging them. A running joke among the black neighbors was, on learning that an unwed girl was pregnant, to suggest that she had gotten the baby at Oddo's because he tried to sell black people everything else. Like the Gaglianos, the Oddos were Italian Americans, but people would sometimes insist that Oddo was Jewish, citing his alleged business practices and mercenary demeanor to counter dissenters from this view. It would be a mistake to understand this stereotyping as reflecting committed anti-Semitism, however, as it would be to take references to the Gaglianos as "dagoes" as indicating actively anti-Italian sentiments.

Anyway, that summer I obtained my first (and, it turned out, last) remote- controlled model airplane. I was quite excited about it but leery of the combination of gasoline engine and whirring propeller that had to be dealt with to fly it. It just seemed that there was a lot involved in that proposition that could go wrong, with serious injury as a result. As it happened, the Gaglianos' son, Tony Jr.—about five or six years my elder, as I recall—was a model plane buff. Probably as the result of a casual conversation with some adult in my family, he came over to help me prepare the plane for flight. We spent much of an afternoon in my backyard with him instructing me and helping me overcome my anxiety. It was an entirely unstrained interaction. He was empathetic and reassuring and encouraging in a manner that I expect a supportive black teenager would have been. We talked a little about our lives, school, sports. When he was confident that I could handle the plane on my own, he left. I thanked him profusely; he said that it was nothing and that he was happy to help me out. I never ran across Tony Jr. again. There was no reason to: he had his life; I had mine. Again, I have no idea what he or his parents would have said if asked to declare themselves about the Jim Crow regime; they very well could have proclaimed it to be the law of God and nature. Yet they were all clearly capable of dealing with black people as they would any other human being they considered as no different from themselves, and they did so spontaneously and without apparent effort.

Within a few years Oddo closed his store and left. Several years later the Gaglianos did the same. The Gaglianos had been at it long enough to want to retire; they'd run the store at least all my life, and who knows how long before. They also had been fretful about competition from the chain supermarkets that had opened not far from our enclave. Black neighbors surmised that they all had made money for a comfortable retirement off black Hollygrove and that the Gaglianos raised their kids and then moved to Metairie like Oddo. They well may have been correct.

Black New Orleanians' views of Jews and Italians under Jim Crow were complicated. Both populations were certainly considered white in all meaningful senses of that classification; yet black people commonly characterized them as at the same time lying somewhere between blacks and whites, typically with the implication that they were, or should be, more sympathetic (or at least less bigoted) because other whites discriminated against them as well. Jews were prominent in the city's philanthropic community, especially those endeavors associated with black racial uplift. The most substantial benefactors, Edgar

Stern and his wife Edith Rosenwald Stern, heiress to the Sears
Roebuck fortune, were primary patrons of black institutions,
notably Dillard University and the Flint-Goodridge Hospital,
and were instrumental in the development of Pontchartrain
Park, one of the first suburban-style housing subdivisions for
blacks in the country. Anti-Semitism in New Orleans was
garden variety—a casual expression of the panoply of petty
stereotypes and exclusion from many of the upper class's social
clubs and voluntary organizations. That is, talk of blood libel
or international Jewish conspiracy was not common, although
militant white supremacists denounced Jews as agents of
race-mixing.

The closest there was to an open effort to mobilize anti-
Semitism politically during the postwar decades didn't get off
the ground and was ironically misplaced. The local Schwegmann Brothers Giant Supermarket chain was a forerunner of
today's big-box stores. Between the late 1940s and the early
1960s it grew to eighteen stores in the area, with the largest a
155,000 square foot location that was at the time the largest
supermarket in the world. As one of its advantages of scale,
Schwegmann's practiced discount pricing, in contravention of
vestigial "fair trade" laws that prohibited the practice. An additional point of comparative advantage was that Schwegmann's
stores opened early on Sundays, breaking with custom rooted
in blue laws, which limited shopping on Sundays. Competi-
tors challenged the discount pricing in court but also objected
to the stores' Sunday schedule as unfair; some denounced
the policy as un-Christian, which was clearly intended as an
anti-Semitic barb, based on the erroneous assumption that
the Schwegmann chain was Jewish-owned. The Schwegmann
family was not Jewish.

Italians were viewed more broadly as not exactly white, perhaps in part because of their own history in the city. Another factor was that the dark-complexioned Sicilians shaded phenotypically into indistinguishability from the black Creole population. Uptown, white upper-class prejudice against Italians persisted at least through most of the twentieth century, to the extent that in 1977 many Uptown whites supported Ernest N. "Dutch" Morial, who became the city's first black mayor, as more palatable racially than Joe Di Rosa, his Italian American opponent.

The textures in the Jim Crow fabric as it was woven in New Orleans convey a sense of how racial segregation as an ideology, a set of official institutions and cast of mind, could be suspended, or at least overlooked temporarily, in the imperfectly chartable realm of personal interaction and daily life, in shared neighborhoods and elsewhere. I don't mean to suggest that these little subversions were unique to New Orleans. On some scale they could have occurred anywhere and almost certainly did in most places with greater or lesser frequency. I do think that they were more likely in places like New Orleans, where the social terrain on which they could occur—the gray area of personal encounter where the codes of subordination's guidelines were less clear and the options more flexible—was larger than in most places and more difficult to avoid.

I also don't mean to exaggerate their significance. To be sure, we were vulnerable to white caprice, unjust laws and unequal enforcement, and all the material inequalities—occupational segregation, overt employment, income, housing, and financial discrimination—that were thus enabled. (I recall boiling with anger on the bus ride home from high school when we passed the hypocrisy chiseled across the Orleans Parish Courthouse portal: "The Impartial Administration of Justice Is the Foundation of Liberty.") We were, by state law, municipal ordinance, and unofficial practice, no better than second-class citizens, and we perceived the role of the police as somewhere between antebellum slave patrols and an occupying army, though without that terminology's pithiness and rhetorical clarity.

Nor would I suggest that those instances of common human recognition were conscious deviations, politically charged moments stolen by conspirators. They were not. If anything, they could exist only as reflexes, well below the radar scope of political consciousness. And they were extremely fragile for that reason. They could easily be undone by political climate changes that extended white supremacy's radar range. One of the schools—then named for Judah P. Benjamin, the Jewish former US senator and later member of Jefferson Davis's Confederate cabinet—targeted in the first wave of desegregation was located in my triangular portion of Hollygrove (which I admit weighs heavily in the picture I paint here of biracial neighborhood life). Within a year of eruption of the school crisis that brought police barricades and riot control dogs as a daily presence, the whites fell prey to blockbusting frenzy, and the neighborhood went from being roughly half and half racially to nearly all black. As has so frequently been the case all over America, white flight made good quality housing stock available to blacks, though no doubt at inflated prices and profits for realtors.

In addition, while these interactions in themselves could be egalitarian, the contexts in which they were enacted, and therefore the terms on which they were approached, were not. White people typically exercised control over what form an interracial interaction would take, whether it would be hostile or cordial, condescending or not, whether it would even occur. A virtue of a big city with relatively loose racial controls was that a response in kind to hostility was less likely to have threatening consequences, and black people tended to take advantage of that latitude. But the background framework was always one in which whites held the trump cards. They faced no danger beyond momentary embarrassment or unpleasant response from potentially saying the wrong thing, and they had no serious reason for wariness on entering an encounter. They could presume a cordial, or at least civil, response; we couldn't, at least not outside those relationships that had built up sediment over time and in relatively neutral, and thus more egalitarian, settings like daily neighborhood life.

Most important, the moments of spontaneously acknowledged commonality that I've described were not typical. They were much less common than white southerners' self-serving accounts would suggest, but more frequent than can be fit into a picture of the segregated South as a nightmare of unremitting degradation and driven by ubiquitous, universally willful bigotry. Nonetheless, it is telling that fleeting instances of unrestrained decency and simple cordiality can loom so large in memory. Far more commonly, whites approached blacks in ways that assumed varying degrees of deference and subordination. Black people by and large accepted that fact and adjusted standards of judgment accordingly. "Mean" or "prejudiced" white people were those who crossed a variable line, a threshold beyond which injuries and insults exceeded the everyday norm and became gratuitous or compounded.

Civility is a relative category; what counts as acceptable treatment in interaction always assumes a broader framework of social hierarchy and the expectations appropriate to one's position within it. Black professionals, for example, were more likely than domestics, laborers, or sharecroppers to balk at being addressed by their first names by whites toward whom they couldn't adopt the same familiarity. This difference in reaction shouldn't suggest that professionals had a more acute sense of injustice than others, though that implication is, and was, commonly enough drawn by middle-class black people themselves and other observers. Instead, it reflected the different social realities of different economic strata. We can see the effects of this difference in a couple of ways that are not mutually exclusive.

An element of the perception of middle-class status is a claim to respectability, based on notions of accomplishment and civic worth and standing. Even in the Jim Crow world middle-class people considered recognition of this claim as an entitlement, if only in forms that did not radically breach the basic conventions of white supremacy. Being addressed as "Mr.," "Mrs.," "Dr.," "Professor," or "Reverend" where appropriate, for instance, would be the ideal. (The more specific professional titles like "Dr." or "Reverend," ironically, seemed less to strain white supremacist etiquette than generic titles "Mr." and "Mrs.," in part because they could be sprinkled around randomly, tongue in cheek, as a minstrel-like mockery of supposed black pretentiousness and tendencies to "put on airs.") But being addressed simply by last name without title was preferable to being called by one's given name, or, worst of all, generic references of servile familiarity like "Uncle" or "Auntie."

Black southerners of all strata understood those demeaning references, as well as the one-sided access to the familiarity of first name address, for what they were—markers that reinscribed in everyday interaction the social order's fundamental principle of racial inequality. Ideological premises associated with class position may have raised the threshold of middle-class black people's expectations of minimal civility. More important, though, were their relatively greater abilities to avoid situations in which they would be condescended to or demeaned by whites, especially in bigger cities. The contexts of their employment were less likely to involve direct white supervision, and their greater economic capacities afforded them more choice in their commercial and consumer interactions.

Others who operated within different circumstances of daily life necessarily maintained lower thresholds of expectation. Their work contexts were much more likely to subject them, as regular, routine experience, to all the forms of interaction with whites that expressed racial dominance and subordination unabashedly. People accept what they must but no worse. The standards of interracial interaction that most black southerners had to accept were certainly farther away from assumption of what segregationist whites denounced as "social equality" than those that middle-class people tried to demand as minimal decency. For instance, most black people quietly endured one-sided first-name address; it was too much a part of daily life to permit them to do otherwise. But the subtle boundaries of tolerance varied with place and time, and they were always contested around the margins. In the postwar South, at least outside rural, plantation areas like the Mississippi Delta, even domestics would reject vestiges of slavery like "Auntie" or "Uncle" as excessive. Workers commonly referred to their white superiors as "Cap," for Captain. This was a compromise that evoked white southerners' older penchant for adorning themselves with Confederate military titles, authentic or affected, but it also circumvented the use of "Sir." (The word "boss" has a similar origin; it came into favor among northern white workers in the early nineteenth century as a less demeaning term than "master." That it was a derivative of "baas," the Dutch term for "master," did not make it a less appealing alternative.) Older black men frequently subverted even this compromise title by using it in friendly address with one another.

In the early 1990s, Bess Watson, a cousin in my father's generation who lived in the hamlet of Eudora, Arkansas, regularly traveled three hours each way to Memphis for cancer treatment. On one of my visits, Bess had recently returned from a treatment and was still fuming because a white nurse's aide had asked her, regarding filling out some form, "Auntie, can you read?" Bess had lived much of her life in Pine Bluff as a public-school teacher and physician's wife, then widow. She retired to Eudora, where she ran the family's mortuary business for the patriarch, my Great-Uncle Clarence, who was himself a product of Tuskegee Institute and Atlanta University. Her interaction with the nurse's aide was of the sort that seems to validate the view that little has changed. But the white woman's presumption was at best vestigial and naïve, at worst an all too contemporary attempt to assert a superiority anchored in the codes of the long since dissolved ancien régime. Bess probably could have gotten her disciplined by her employer for having asked the question.

By definition, people who are oppressed know it. It strains logic to imagine how one could not notice being brutalized, demeaned, and denied effective recourse. A crucial error made by exuberant radicals at least since the 1960s has been assuming that their discovery of exploitation and oppression must also be fresh news to more beleaguered victims. The Black Panther Party's dogma, in the late 1960s and early 1970s, that political mobilization requires first demonstrating the reign of police terror in urban bantustans, or other Black Powerites' conviction that black Americans needed to be told that they were black are striking cases in point. This is why they could be so easily caricatured in blaxploitation films of the time as ineffectual and out of touch with the realities of popular black existence and why their exhortations and preachments, and others in that vein, have so commonly met only bemused responses. They self-righteously announce the obvious and offer only unthinkably remote, millennial routes to justice like "revolution" or "unity" (or now, reparations).

It would be even more absurd to suggest that black southerners could have been blind to the fundamental injustice of the ways that a system of inequality as blunt and upfront as the Jim Crow order infiltrated and shaped every interaction, every life step. Yet people make daily life under any conditions, even in such extreme circumstances as maximum-security prisons, Nazi concentration camps, Palestinian refugee camps, long-term military occupation, or even chattel slavery. We devise, improvise, and adapt local systems of meaning and value, and the customs, practices, and behavior—including personal habits—that cement them, to enable us to find dignity and worth, solace and respite, even within the boundaries imposed on those at the bottom of systems of extreme, rigidly enforced inequality. Among the relatively weak and powerless in such systems, at least tacit awareness of the fundamental injustice shapes all social interactions. It is part of the natural

environment, the backdrop against which one crafts perceptions of oneself and others, notions of satisfaction and comfort,
accomplishment and worth, pleasure and desire—all the more
so when no plausible remedies seem available.

Even in those areas in the South where white supremacy
was enforced most blatantly and ruthlessly, racial oppression
did not occupy all of black people's mental and social lives.
This is a point that novelist Ralph Ellison, for instance, made
forcefully in his novel *Invisible Man*, as well as repeatedly, and
eloquently, in his social and cultural essays. Black southerners
sought to create social and personal spaces in which they could
express and realize themselves outside, or, as much as possible, within the narrow limits imposed by segregation. Church
and recreational activities, kin and friendship networks, and
lodges or other voluntary associations, as well as purely solitary,
individual pursuits provided spaces for stepping temporarily
outside the boundaries of the social order's enforced racial roles.
The Jim Crow system could disappear momentarily across the
horizon of consciousness in a lodge meeting, church service,
an informal social gathering, or a hobby. In those spaces it was
possible to express oneself with relative freedom, to exhibit
qualities like leadership, mastery of organizational or other
forms of specialized knowledge, and dignified social status—
features of citizenship—that were denied to black people in
the South's official political and economic life.

At the same time, segregated black communities were not
as depicted in Toni Morrison's novels. They were not organic,
self-contained societies. Whites' power—any white person's
power—over livelihood, life, and death never disappeared
entirely from the picture. Nor did the system's economic and
legal constraints.

Black southerners also typically tried as much as possible to protect themselves from the arbitrary political and economic discipline of a system in which the fundamental systemic objective was securing and stabilizing ruling class power. That objective magnified the attractiveness of economic independence or autonomy, through land ownership, for example, and other avenues of self-employment or employment free of direct white supervision. It underlay the Exoduster migrations out of what later would be called the Deep South (the construct didn't come into usage until the 1930s or 1940s) and to the Arkansas Delta region after the Civil War and other attempts to found all-black towns in the nineteenth century. Even the sharecrop system had developed out of these concerns to avoid direct supervision. Sharecropping was an arrangement in which farmers contracted with planters to produce crops in exchange for a "furnish" of equipment and supplies and a claim to a portion of the crop, minus the costs of the "furnish." This system made it possible to organize agricultural labor by individual households, without a white boss or overseer, and it held out the promise of greater opportunities for attaining economic independence. This promise was seldom realized, however, as the planters' much greater economic and political power and the denial of blacks' citizenship rights—as well as the precariousness of the cotton economy and its cash-strapped planters—stacked the deck against farmers' efforts.

The desire for insulation from the Jim Crow order's limits also has fueled the recurrence of more ambitious dreams of collective autonomy or independence. Support for Marcus Garvey's agitation for black economic independence in the 1920s and other less ideologically flamboyant schemes for developing insular local, or national, economies based on racial solidarity attest to its persistence. With the partial exception of Garveyism, these schemes did not generate broad support. And all fizzled, largely because they have come up against two fatal obstacles.

One is that segregated black communities were not separate reservations; they were excluded from political and civic life, not southern economic life. The point was not to remove them from the mainstream economy but to enforce their subordinate position within it. Cultivation of a separate racial economy would require degrees of political independence and resources to protect industries and regulate markets that were unthinkable, especially in a context in which black people could not anticipate having any political rights at all. These dreams could rely on little more than moral appeals to racial solidarity, which were no match for more competitive prices and wages offered from outside. Lack of political rights also meant that black business ventures had no defenses against hostile white actions against them—from terrorist attacks to ostensibly legal means, such as targeting their locations for demolition in the name of urban renewal or harassment through invidious enforcement of public codes and ordinances.

The second obstacle is simple and straight-forward, though proponents of the dream of a separate economy have never accepted it. The vast majority of black Americans, in the South and elsewhere, have shown themselves repeatedly to be much less interested in elaborate programs of separate development than in securing equal opportunity and justice in the here-and-now. Most people respond favorably to appeals to racial pride and solidarity, to be sure. And, within reasonable limits of convenience, cost, and quality, many will patronize black-owned businesses when they can. Even under segregation, however, that commitment was rarely dogmatic. Black people have not proven willing to commit themselves in substantial numbers to long-term projects that seem like pursuit of pie-in-the-sky, least of all, perhaps, when the principal benefit promised is being able to identify vicariously with others who would actually consume the dreamed-for pie.

The objective of escaping white authority is an area where class differences among black people were particularly meaningful. Middle-class people were better able to create buffers between themselves and their families and the worst, most dangerous features of the Jim Crow order. It's no accident, for example, that I've said nothing about my childhood years in Pine Bluff in discussing interracial interaction. Not counting the German nuns and priests at my school and an occasional faculty member at the black college where my father taught, I can recall only one encounter with a white person there, at a small store not far from my school. My parents judged that a young white woman, perhaps one of the proprietors, who worked there was too casual in her interactions with blacks, to the point of being "frisky" or coquettish. After accompanying them on one visit, they instructed me never to go there alone. I never entered the store again. This was no more than two or three years after Emmett Till's murder.

Like many families in many places, my family in New Orleans determined which department stores and other white establishments we would patronize largely on the basis of assessments of the degrees of racial indignity the competing alternatives imposed. Occasionally, an easy choice demanded no humiliating concessions of black customers. A men's clothing store, Porter's, was one such place, and it had a Mexican sales manager who was quite friendly with my grandfather. We bought almost all our menswear there. For the most part, though, it was necessary to make imperfect choices: was it a greater affront to be denied the right to try on hats or shoes? (Some stores permitted neither; those, of course, we scorned at all costs.) The calculus of tolerance differed for different people, of course. Some stores that others found acceptable, we refused to enter, and vice versa. Some people would mix and match preferences, as we did, to preserve dignity as much as possible. We bought shoes here, hats there; equitable treatment was at least as important as style and bargains. And some pleasures were seductive and delightful enough to justify occasionally trying to screen out the distasteful context of enjoyment, providing that the requirements weren't gratuitously humiliating. I recall the strawberry fountain sodas at McCrory's Five & Dime on Canal Street, which could be obtained only at the segregated lunch counter, as one such exception.

Ability to stand on principle in this way was not only enhanced by being in a big city with a variety of options; being able to choose among those options was also dependent on class and income. Most black people were poor enough— this was the point of the system, after all—that, as a practical matter, those options didn't exist. And the class experience of segregation differed in other ways as well, arguably more significant but less apparent to a relatively privileged child or teen.

The more common black experience was dominated by extreme financial insecurity; jobs marked by arbitrary or brutal labor discipline; income that could afford little better than hand-to-mouth existence; and demeaning, arduous, and dangerous conditions of employment with no prospects for improvement or advancement. Public institutions designated for blacks were woefully underfunded, and all separate facilities for blacks were designed to be markedly inferior in quality.

In plantation districts the school year was often truncated to fit the cycles of the cotton crop.

In Pine Bluff some students who attended my school were bused in from rural areas in the county. I knew vaguely that they were understood by other students to be a group distinct from the rest of us and that they were also sometimes the targets of disparaging references. They were clearly poorer than other students, though few students were well-off, not even by the modest standards accessible to the local black middle class. More commonly than among others, one or another of the rural students couldn't attend school for lack of shoes or a coat, and they wore obviously hand-me-down clothes. After some time I noticed that they didn't show up in school until the third or fourth week of classes each year, and they stopped attending about a month before the rest of us. When I asked why, my parents explained to me that their families were share-croppers and that the planters in the county wouldn't permit the school buses to operate during peak times in the cotton season—planting, picking, chopping—when all hands of all ages were needed in the fields.

Middle-class "respectable" people sought as much as possible also to insulate themselves and their children from contact with blacks considered to be class inferiors. An elaborate structure of social clubs—for example, the Links and the Girl Friends for women, the Boulé for men, Jack and Jill for children, and the college alumni fraternity and sorority chapters—evolved to create and sustain homogeneous middle-class social net-works locally and nationally. Segregation did have a leveling effect within the race. Upper-status people were forced to share neighborhoods, schools, and often churches, restaurants, and other public entertainments with those they'd prefer not to associate with. From the system's beginnings a complaint about the injustice of enforced segregation was that it didn't provide for class distinctions among black people. An element of Plessy's brief, as plaintiff in the 1896 Supreme Court case, was that it denied "respectable" black people the right to first-class accommodations and lumped them together with their social inferiors. Militant early opponents of Jim Crow, such as Anna Julia Cooper, often identified as an early black feminist activist, and the young W. E. B. Du Bois were among the more well-known people who voiced this objection felt more widely within their nascent class.

As is often noted, outward trappings of affluence could stoke white hostility, provoking charges of "uppityness." In that circumstance signs of black material attainment could be hazardous. And the regime's arbitrariness meant that even in cities, where class distinctions among black people were more likely to be recognized and tolerated by whites, middle-class social position and connections couldn't necessarily be relied upon to divert the system's horrors. A friend of mine in high school, whose father was a junior high school teacher and had been a high school and college classmate of my mother, had a moment of youthful indiscretion not much more serious than my shoplifting escapade. Shortly before his sixteenth birthday he went for a joyride with some neighborhood friends who had stolen a car. They were caught by the police. He looked a good bit older than his years, and, perhaps for that reason or maybe to make an example of him or maybe just because they could do it, the District Attorney's office tried him as an adult. No attempted intercession by his parents could help. He was convicted and sentenced to time at Angola. Within a year we heard that he was dead.

Nevertheless, middle-class black people were better able than others to shield themselves from both the everyday indignities and the atrocities of the Jim Crow world. And their social status and economic position typically derived from occupying niches that were provided by and that accommodated to the segregationist order. The principal sources of middle-class status and relative economic security came from jobs in the segregated institutions whose main purpose was to give a façade to the lie of separate but equal. The black middle class was anchored occupationally in teaching in and administering the segregated school systems or operating businesses that serviced segregated markets—restaurants, motels, beauty and barber shops, funeral parlors—or that could take advantage of racial solidarity. Professions like medicine, dentistry, law, the building trades, and the ministry were the most common among these, but, apart from the clergy, they were concentrated in the bigger cities. South Carolina had only one black lawyer as late as 1950. Other jobs that may have involved service to whites or more direct white supervision but that promised a steady, better-than-subsistence income—for example, employment as dining car waiters, sleeping car porters, and longshore workers, who like many of the tradesmen had union benefits and protections, postal workers, or other federal jobs—were another staple of the black middle class. We were all unequal, but some were more unequal and unprotected than others. And these differences in social position would prove to have significant impact on the shaping of black politics after the segregationist regime's demise and, therefore, on the character of the new southern politics that has emerged in its aftermath.

2

The Order in Flux and Being in Flux within the Order

I have tried to present a picture of the everyday realities of life under the Jim Crow order, at least in a couple of contexts. Several recollected incidents, more than thirty years apart, may help to sharpen this picture. They also may be revealing in multiple ways—about past and present, how perception and recollection can differ with social position and how the racial etiquette of Jim Crow could vary.

In 1965, I rode a Trailways bus from Pine Bluff to New Orleans. To put the date into proper perspective, it was less than a year and a half after the murders of James Chaney, Andrew Goodman, and Michael Schwerner in Philadelphia, Mississippi (recounted in the bizarre 1980s film, *Mississippi Burning*) and a few months after the murder of Viola Liuzzo during the Selma voting rights campaign. My (and my parents') main anxiety about this trip was that it required three changes of bus: one in Monroe, Louisiana; another in Alexandria, Louisiana; and the last in Baton Rouge. Monroe was the specific concern; it was a citadel of segregationist resistance in the Delta region of northeast Louisiana, and I had recently

grown my first beard, which could have marked me as a possible civil rights worker.

I decided to handle the trip by slumping into the very last
seat on the bus with a book and a pint of cheap vodka that I
would sip from all the way. It was holiday season, and on the
first leg of the trip a lively group of students from black colleges in Little Rock, Pine Bluff, and elsewhere were spread out
over the half-empty bus, passing the time playing cards and
talking convivially. I didn't attempt to join in, partly because
I was tired, partly because the students engaged mainly in
groups of schoolmates, and I was a stranger to them all. Two
hours or so out of Pine Bluff, late at night, the bus stopped at
Lake Village, Arkansas, in Chicot County in the Delta. I knew
much of what there was to know about Lake Village because
it's a few miles from Eudora, the small town near the Louisiana
border where my Arkansas family has roots.

In Lake Village an elderly, infirm white couple boarded the
bus. The driver stood and instructed the two black students
sitting directly behind him to get up and give their seats to the
couple, even though there were several vacant pairs of seats
immediately behind them that would have imposed no greater
difficulty on the couple. The two students refused, and others
called out their support and protested the driver's demand.
He held firm and after a couple of moments of tense stand-
off threatened to call the sheriff. Segregation on public transit
had been outlawed several years earlier, but that night in Lake
Village there were no federal courts or marshals, no AP report-
ers, no one except us and him.

As I sat in my seat with my vodka bottle, I recalled that,
during the search for the bodies of Schwerner, Goodman, and
Chaney, the bodies of two young black men, Charles Moore

and Henry Dee, were discovered in a bayou near Tallulah, Louisiana, roughly an hour south of Lake Village and an hour east from Monroe, our destination. They were both twenty-one years old; Moore was a student at black Alcorn College. Neither had been active in the civil rights movement, and both had disappeared—unreported and unremarked upon. Another body, of a black teenager who was never identified, was found floating in the Big Black River in Mississippi. These discoveries were treated as afterthoughts or false alarms, just as black Mississippian James Chaney's demise would have been treated had he not been accompanied by the two white, northern college students. The victims weren't given names at first and wouldn't have been noticed at all were it not for the initial mistaken identity and the fact that national attention was focused on the other search. Their stories faded from the national spotlight almost instantly. Moore and Dee had been abducted and killed by the Klan in a Mississippi forest preserve; two Klansmen were eventually charged for the murders, but the state of Mississippi refused to prosecute them. No investigation was ever conducted into the death of the unidentified teen, who was wearing a Congress of Racial Equality T-shirt, and we still have no idea how, why, or by whom he was killed. I realized how easily the dozen or so of us on that bus could have disappeared in like manner that night.

The students didn't back down. The bus driver stood at the front of the bus and surveyed us all. Then, for whatever reasons, without another word he returned to his seat and continued on his route. He may have been tired and preferred to avoid the hassle and delay of dealing with the cops. He may have appreciated that he had no legal basis for his command. He may have calculated that it would have been too difficult to explain the absence of so many passengers, whether we were simply incarcerated in Chicot County or killed and our bodies disposed of. Luckily, when we arrived in Monroe, another of the north Louisiana segregationist hellholes, my connection was already in the station, so I spent only a very few anxious minutes moving from one bus to the next, tense and holding my breath until I slouched, with my bottle, in the relatively safe obscurity of another last seat. We reached Alexandria, on the border of the calmer, south Louisiana Acadiana district, where I also had the assurance of relatives in town, shortly after sunrise. I had a cup of coffee in the station and felt a measure of relief, though I stiffened when we made our one stop before Baton Rouge, in the small, Avoyelles Parish town of Bunkie.

That was my last time on the ground in that area for nearly three decades. In the mid-1990s I took a few days to drive around and hang out in the Delta region of Arkansas, Louisiana, and Mississippi. It was at the end of cotton picking and ginning season, and the red stalks and snowy white bolls still were prominent in the fields and adorned the highway. I stopped for lunch at a roadside restaurant in Lake Village. On the way out, after an unexceptional hamburger and unexceptionally casual and cordial interaction with the white waitress and cashier, I noticed on the bulletin board next to the entrance an announcement of a function sponsored by the antimilitarist Chicot County Peace Action Council.

A few months after the harrowing bus trip, in 1966, I once again traveled from Pine Bluff to New Orleans, this time by plane. I had been informed by the ticket agent that my itinerary went through El Dorado, but I didn't know that that meant I had to change planes there. You can imagine how unprepared I was to find myself and my suitcase deposited on the tarmac as the DC-3 barely stopped taxiing to discharge me.

El Dorado is a small city in extreme south-central Arkansas, close to the Louisiana border, about forty miles from Monroe. It's in the oil-producing area that launched ultrareactionary billionaire H. L. Hunt. As I tried to get my bearings while standing on the tarmac, I could see drilling rigs and pumps, working with their languorous rhythm, dotting the flat landscape. It was a Sunday afternoon, either Palm Sunday or Easter, and, though the day was strikingly clear and sunny, an uncommonly brisk breeze filled the air.

There were no signs of life outside the small terminal, and the afternoon was absolutely quiet, save for the distant, faint sound of the oil pumps. I entered the restraining gate and approached the terminal to settle in for my almost three-hour lay-over. As I drew nearer the terminal, I realized that there were two entrances, at either end of the building. Because it was two years after segregation had been outlawed in all public accommodations, there were no signs over the entrances to indicate who was supposed to use which, but I knew what the story was. I looked inside the terminal for telltale signs—black people in the cluster of waiting area seats at one end of the building, whites at the other. There wasn't a living soul visible inside the building either.

So then I had a serious choice to make. Should I gamble on going through the proper door? The cost of a wrong guess could have been zero; it could be that the terminal had been integrated without incident and that no one would care which door I entered. But the cost of a mistake could have been everything. I was alone in an unfamiliar place where I didn't know the local norms. I don't think even my parents knew that I was going to deplane in El Dorado, not that it would've made any difference if they had. If I'd run across the wrong individuals on the wrong day or given off the wrong vibes, I could have disappeared and been dropped, without a trace, into the Ouachita River.

I pondered the situation long and hard. Then I sat on a bench outside and read in the cold, sharp wind until my connecting flight arrived from Dallas.

In 1968, the film *The Boston Strangler*, starring Tony Curtis as Albert DeSalvo, the gas company meter reader generally believed to have been the actual Boston killer, opened in Chapel Hill, North Carolina, where I attended college. The case had become a national sensation because it was one of the early instances of what would later be known as serial murder to receive broad television news exposure. Interest was heightened because the killings continued for months after Boston authorities and the media began blanketing the city with alerts, including the fact that the homes of the victims—all women—showed no signs of forcible entry. Apparently, the culprit was so disarming that he charmed his way into the homes of his prey even when they were forewarned. (Much of the speculation about his continued success in gaining entry traded on stereotypes of women's gullibility or susceptibility to flattery and, after police surmised that he may have been assisted by official credentials of some sort, their weakness for men in uniforms.) Two spree killing events that had gained national notoriety only two years earlier—Richard Speck's murder of eight student nurses in Chicago and Charles Whitman's murder of seventeen people in Austin, Texas—no doubt contributed to an environment conducive to popular hysteria.

The story also had local significance because a few years earlier the university had been the site of a murder, unsolved to this day, of a white female student in the arboretum on campus. That case was already a prominent element of ghoulish student lore. Although the murder had no witnesses, and no serious suspects were ever identified, speculation persisted that the killer may have been black, notwithstanding an initial report of a freckled, redheaded, middle-aged white man seen emerging from the arboretum with blood on his hands, shirt, and neck. The basis for the speculation was that the police claimed to have found "negroid hairs" at the crime scene.

It was also a time of general upheaval on campus. The university and town—there was hardly a distinction between the two—were coming off a period of intense civil rights activism, complete with sit-ins and ugly resistance, and anti-war protests were accelerating. Women had only recently begun attending the university as first-year undergraduates, and strict curfew restrictions on them were being relaxed as a result of student power agitation. The student population that had entered college with the frame of mind and aspirations characteristic of the late 1950s was being transformed before its own eyes into the orientations and ways of life representing what would be identified as the 1960s. The first syllables of the language of women's liberation were already faintly audible, and the number of black students on campus quadrupled in a year and doubled again the next.

This context is clear only in retrospect. That's one reason I was taken so completely by surprise by what happened. *The Boston Strangler* drew heavy attendance. It seems that the film ran at the downtown theater for at least a week, but that may not be correct; it may have seemed to run forever because, once I realized what was going on, I couldn't wait for it to leave. It set off a wave of hysteria among white female students. Sensational, and unbelievable, reports of attempted assaults—all by unidentified, and, fortunately, undescribed, black men—occurred almost daily while the film remained on the marquee. Two stand out for being improbable to the point of preposterousness.

One student claimed that she woke up in her dorm room in the middle of the night to find a black man standing over her menacingly. She screamed, and the man disappeared before her roommate, who was awakened by her scream, could see him. Women's dorms, even with the relaxed curfew rules, were on very tight security. No intruder could have entered the dorm undetected, and there were no signs of forcible entry. Unless he had magical powers, he couldn't have escaped without the roommate seeing him or his being seen by someone else in the dorm. The story was clearly a bad dream that overtook reality.

The second story was maybe even less credible. The next day another student reported being grabbed outside her dorm at three in the afternoon by a vaguely described black man who attempted to drag her behind bushes near the dorm's entrance. This dorm faced onto the busiest street that ran through the campus. The "bushes" were two thin shrubs, three feet high and two feet wide at the top but much narrower at the trunk, that flanked the three or four steps to the dorm's front door. Only the most suicidally insane person would have attempted so hopeless an assault, and any such attempt, particularly by a black man on a white female student, would have been noticed by the knot of pedestrian and automobile traffic on that street every afternoon.

I don't know whether the campus or town police recognized these reports as hysteria and chose discreetly not to dismiss them publicly as what they so clearly were. I didn't hear about any black students or town residents being arrested or questioned about them. I was reminded at the time of a case a few years earlier, when I was in high school in New Orleans. A young white woman reported having been raped by a black man one night in City Park. After several days during which she failed to finger any of the possible suspects the New Orleans Police Department presented to her, she broke down and admitted her hoax. She had been stood up in the park by her sailor boyfriend and concocted the story to make him feel guilty. Meanwhile, there's no telling how many young black men vaguely matching her vague description had been snatched off the streets and terrorized by police. At least she was decent enough not to persist any longer with her hoax.

A year after the episode sparked by *The Boston Strangler*, a white student with whom I was friendly was abducted from downtown Chapel Hill and raped by a black man with whom she was passingly acquainted. He was a hanger-on at a bar and restaurant many of us frequented. She was an activist in the anti-war movement and the budding women's liberation movement on campus and was very sensitive to the seriousness of the charge of black-on-white rape. Immediately after the incident she came to talk to me and a good friend, also black, who was a graduate student, seeking advice on whether to report the assault to the police. She was concerned that filing charges would reinforce the ugly racial stereotype and force her to participate in the unfairness of the criminal justice system by heaping an extreme punishment on her rapist. After some discussion we both told her that, while we certainly appreciated and sympathized with her reservations, rape was rape, and that she should report the incident, if only because the perpetrator would be likely to do it again to any woman, without regard to race. Eventually she did report the crime, but with very ambivalent feelings about her action.

One morning in 1970, I was walking with my pregnant wife along Hay Street, the main drag in downtown Fayetteville, North Carolina. Fayetteville then was a city of about 50,000 people, a third or more of them black, located at the point where the Piedmont shades into the Coastal Plain. At that time, it was outnumbered and at least figuratively surrounded by a party of soldiers and airmen at nearby Fort Bragg and Pope Air Force base more than one and a half times as large as the city's population. Bragg was home to the 82nd Airborne Division, 18th Airborne Corps, JFK School of Special Warfare, and US Army Special Forces. It had also been until recently a basic training center for new recruits. We had moved there as part of an organizing project centered on providing civilian support to anti-war GIs at Bragg. Our project, which was staffed mainly by people who knew and had worked with one another in student, anti-war, community, and labor organizing in the state, was funded by the United States Servicemen's Fund that supported the anti-war coffeehouses associated with the GI anti-war movement.

Our project raised some eyebrows and was met with skepticism, if not consternation, by a number of those working on existing projects because we determined from the very beginning that the nature of racial division at Bragg and in Fayetteville was such that we should have distinct black and white nodes, though we worked collaboratively. (At the opposite end of the continuum, the Camp Pendleton project was run by a doctrinaire sectarian group, led by a dour white male and Asian American female couple referred to derisively by others in the movement as Socialist Man and Socialist Woman. They traveled with a pair of Marines, one black and the other white, projected as embodying interracial proletarian solidarity, but who seemed more like Gladys Knight's Pips.) Our two loci were the Haymarket Square Coffeehouse, named for its location and also a play on the more famous site of the 1886 Haymarket police riot in Chicago, near downtown Fayetteville, and the Mbari Cultural Center in a black business district near the historically black Fayetteville State University. For several years before our arrival, a local Quaker House had been performing some of those support services for anti-war GIs. Moving to Fayetteville was my swan song to campus-based organizing; my wife, Barbara, had relocated from Wellesley College, where she was in a graduate art history program after having been an art student in New Orleans, where she also did some set design work for Student Non-Violent Coordinating Committee's Free Southern Theater.

Fayetteville was the biggest city at the entrance to eastern North Carolina, historically the state's plantation and Black Belt region, where white supremacist domination was harshest. The city exemplified that politics with a zest. A billboard on the major north-south interstate highway at the edge of town featured a portrait of hooded Klansmen and the legend "The United Klans of America Welcomes You to Fayetteville." Moreover, Fayetteville had a statewide reputation for white supremacist unabashedness because the city license tag (most cities in the state didn't even issue local plates with symbols) was embossed with the town's logo: a likeness of the preserved slave market around which the modern arterial system revolved as the heart of downtown. After I moved there, I learned that preserving that perverse monument to slavery's history had required more of a commitment than I'd imagined. It had been destroyed by Union troops in the Civil War; afterward the city fathers rebuilt it to commemorate their Lost Cause and send an intimidating message to the freed black population.

We'd resided in Fayetteville only a few months when on that morning I happened to jostle an elderly white man as we passed on Hay Street. We brushed shoulders with some force on the not-so-crowded sidewalk. I was startled by this accidental pedestrian collision, but, on looking back at him over my shoulder after he'd passed, I realized that the accident wasn't an accident at all. As he stood a few yards from us and raised the umbrella that he carried as a camouflaged cane, it became clear that this frail old man had chosen our encounter to make a statement. I was supposed to move out of his way on the sidewalk, and he was incensed at my insolence in not having done so. He was so irate, and perhaps overwhelmed and disoriented by the crumbling of the old regime under which any minimally respectable white person could expect automatic and servile deference from any black person anywhere, any time, and in any situation, that he had decided, then and there, to take his stand. His accustomed world was collapsing before his eyes. Already one black person had been elected to the five-member City Council, and white elites complained fulsomely of the unfairness of the black "bloc vote." Moreover, a black poor people's organization with more than two thousand dues-paying members regularly descended on council meetings with raucous, Black Power-style protests.

He brandished the umbrella menacingly and shouted a threat. I cursed him and turned away to resume our walk. Then we noticed that he had begun following us, no doubt intent on teaching me a lesson that he had forgotten could no longer be taught. Suddenly, I was overtaken by imagining, if he would now in his enfeebled state pursue physical confrontation with a man half a century younger and bigger and stronger than he, what horrors—large and small—he must have been capable of imagining or perpetrating when he was younger and more vigorous and when responding to him in kind could have resulted in certain death. Almost without thought I slowed my gait to assist his decrepit pursuit and taunted him to egg him on. I determined on the spot to lure him into the deep alcove of an empty storefront and coax him into swinging his umbrella at me. I was set to beat him into the concrete, right there in that alcove, the equivalent of taking him into a back alley, as a partial repayment for all that he and his ilk had done and had been able to do for so long with impunity. So he was a stooped, shriveled, puny old man? All the better, I felt; lack of competent resistance would permit a more clinically precise beating. My wife was as stunned at my response as at his reaction. Fortunately for us both, he either snapped out of his nostalgic delusions or dropped his bluff. He stopped, turned around, and shuffle-marched away, probably reassured that he had upheld white supremacist principle. For several years before and more than a decade after that encounter, in most of my interactions with white southerners who would have been fully adult during the old regime—and younger whites who had been my contemporaries in New Orleans—I found myself wondering how they might have lived it.

The following year, recently elected Representative Ron Dellums (D-CA) came to Fayetteville on a tour of military stockades. We had arranged for him to give a talk to a meeting of the Fayetteville Area Poor People's Organization, with whom we worked closely, in one of the local public housing projects. After a convivial dinner of fried chicken and potato salad on the living room floor of our house, Congressman Dellums, his key staff aide, and a couple other of us left for the meeting at Cross Creek Court. Traveling through downtown, we went through a yellow light at a major intersection. A police car pulled us over, and one of the two young white cops came up to the driver, a friend who had come over from Chapel Hill and whose car bore a Louisiana plate, and accosted him by saying, "Bo', don't they have yellow lights down there in Louisiana?" My hunch was that neither cop was likely local and that they were probably fairly recent products of the military's Project Transition, which was intended to ease veterans into civilian occupations. One of Project Transition's most famous black beneficiaries was a local dry cleaner whom I've always suspected was at least one model for Norman Lear's George Jefferson.

It struck me that the aggressive cop was young and non-southern enough that he found himself caught between saying "boy" and the Project Transition training that stressed maintaining at least the appearance of nondiscrimination in encounters with civilians. Indeed, over the next few years it was common enough to see police officers taking sociology or even black studies courses at community colleges, partly in pursuit of step or grade increases in pay, but partly to encourage greater sensitivity—or, as my friends and I assumed, to learn how to make class distinctions—in dealings with non-white civilians. At any rate, Dellums launched into a fiery impromptu lecture from the car's back seat about the racial presumptuousness and unacceptability of the officer's approach

to us. All the while he was rifling through his pockets trying
to locate his congressional immunity badge, which he must
have left at his hotel. Fortunately, the other cop who, while
still young, seemed somewhat more seasoned and may even
have gotten word that a black congressman was going to be
in town, moved in to defuse the situation and offered at least
feigned apology for his partner's exuberance. When we got to
the meeting shortly thereafter, Dellums began his remarks by
indicating that he'd had an experience on the way there that
reminded him that in the eyes of the police, without the protections of his office, he was "just another nigger." Whenever
he and I ran into each other over the subsequent years, we
reminisced about that incident.

In the spring of 1974 I traveled from Atlanta, where we had
moved in the summer of 1972 mainly for me to begin graduate school, to a conference in West Point, Mississippi. The
trip was harrowing. We flew, in a DC-3 incapable of flying
above the weather system, through a huge band of violent
storms that spawned tornadoes from the Great Lakes to the
Gulf Coast and killed three hundred people or more, destroy-
ing the campus of Central State University, a historically black
institution in Wilberforce, Ohio. We made two stops, both in
Mississippi—Columbus, where a tornado hit while we were
en route, and Meridian.

   After two days of panels and strategy sessions on the problem
of diminishing black land ownership in the South, the conference was adjourned. I was flying standby, so I left early for
the Columbus airport to increase my chances of getting a seat
on the afternoon flight back to Atlanta. I arrived at the terminal pleased to see that there was no line at the Southern

Airways ticket counter. I stood at the counter and waited for the agent, whom I could see sitting in a rear office handling papers, to notice me so that we could conduct my transaction. After several minutes he raised his head and glanced in my direction, then lowered it again and returned to his papers. I assumed that he had a pressing backlog of paperwork and continued to wait patiently, confident that he'd noticed me and would come to the counter as soon as he was sufficiently caught up to do so.

Then it happened. After several more minutes of waiting, I was joined at the counter by a white man in a suit. Instantly, the agent rose from his desk and scampered to the ticket counter. He went immediately to the white man and asked how he might be of help. The snub couldn't have been more obvious. Without thinking, I cried, "Wait a minute." The ticket agent fixed me with a cutting stare. Then I looked around. The only other black person in the terminal was the elderly janitor, who continued sweeping, looking toward the floor, through the entire incident. Our eyes locked for no more than two or three very meaningful seconds. What he communicated in that moment, or what it seemed to me he was, was basically the following: "Do what you want, but remember that this is Mississippi. I have to live here, and I didn't see anything."

I swallowed my protest and waited quietly until the ticket agent had satisfied his white customer. In a tense, terse inter-action, I conducted my transaction and took a seat. I was very relieved when other nonlocal conference attendees began to trickle into the airport. I was even more relieved to board the plane for my departure.

Three other incidents that year and the year before, all involving encounters with police, highlight the quotidian transition taking place in the region's racial politics. (Much larger instances of transition were taking place across the region, all directly traceable to the impact of the 1965 Voting Rights Act. For example, in 1972 Andrew Young became the first black congressional representative from the South elected in the twentieth century, and the following year Maynard Jackson was elected mayor of Atlanta.) In the first, on a drive from Atlanta to New Orleans in the spring of 1973 to attend a conference and visit family, I was stopped late at night on a desolate stretch of I-65 about halfway between Montgomery and Mobile, Alabama. The (white) state trooper had clocked my speed at more than twenty miles over the speed limit and called me back to his vehicle. In addition, my car had a temporary Georgia license plate, and I still had a North Carolina driver's license. I explained that I was traveling from Atlanta to New Orleans and wanted to make it through before getting too tired. I sat in the passenger seat anxiously waiting for what might happen. The officer coughed, covered his mouth, and said, "Excuse me, sir." Then he told me, very courteously, that he was going to let me go with a warning and instructed me not to speed any more in Alabama.

The second encounter was also late at night and somewhat later that year. My family and I were traveling to the South Carolina Low Country, where I had a meeting; we planned a weekend outing. When we lived in Atlanta, we occasionally took weekend trips to Charleston, which seemed a little like a vest-pocket version of New Orleans. On this trip, instead of taking a more direct route via mainly two-lane highways, including a closely monitored stretch through the eerie Savannah River Plant, a federal nuclear reservation, we went considerably out of the way to stay on interstate highways all the way. We drove north on I-85 to connect with I-26 near Greenville, South Carolina. On I-385, the connecting road between the two interstates, I noticed a car tracking about a quarter mile or so behind me for what seemed like quite a while. I could see no more than its headlights, but I suspected it may have been a state trooper and maintained a steady speed near the limit. Just as I turned onto the ramp connecting to I-26, the car's flashing lights came on. Summoned back to the state trooper's vehicle, I learned in an unnerving way why the front passenger's seat is known as the shotgun seat. I found myself staring into the barrel of a shotgun affixed under the glove box.

The trooper acknowledged that he'd followed me for eight miles and that I hadn't exceeded the speed limit, at least not enough to warrant his giving me a ticket. It turned out that he had followed and stopped me because of a bumper sticker on the car. The sticker read simply "Boycott" with the Gulf Oil logo. The Gulf Boycott was organized by the Pan-African Liberation Committee and other groups in support of the anti-colonial insurgencies in Portuguese Africa. Portugal was engaged in wars in its three colonies—Guinea-Bissau, Angola, and Mozambique. Angola's Cabinda province had substantial oil deposits, and Gulf paid the Portuguese government for drilling rights and protection and thus funded Portugal's war. The boycott was intended to draw attention to Gulf's role. The trooper simply wanted me to explain the bumper sticker to him. So in the middle of the night and the middle of nowhere on a South Carolina roadside, while staring into the barrel of a shotgun, I had to give an impromptu account of the persistence of Portuguese colonialism in Africa and Gulf's complicity in sustaining it. The trooper was attentive and clearly wanted to make sense of it all. Our encounter occurred during the oil crisis induced by the OPEC embargo; in an intended gesture of empathy, he remarked on the difficulties those "*A*-rabs" were causing for us. And he asked whether I was exercised by Gulf and the Portuguese because "they're doing this to your race of people." He also asked, however, where I was going in the state and what the nature of my visit was.

In late spring of 1974, I made another night drive to New Orleans, that time unplanned and for an unhappy occasion. My maternal grandfather had had a stroke not long after his eightieth birthday and was hospitalized in Covington, Louisiana. He had retired roughly a decade earlier from his job as warehouse manager and Spanish-language sales representative for a building supplies company, and he and my grandmother moved, at her behest, to their summer house in that small city—its population in the 1950s was roughly 6,000—on the north shore of Lake Pontchartrain. (As I mention above, Covington has its small place in civil rights history because it was Plessy's destination on the trip he, the Comité des Citoyens, and the East Louisiana Railroad intended to be the basis for a challenge to the state's 1890 Separate Car Act.)

I recalled the summer house from before it was a summer house. It had been a small farm occupied by my grandmother's uncle and aunts, all of whom died in the 1950s. My earliest visits there stood out because (a) there were farm animals—I recall a tremendous sow, some barnyard fowl, and a mule—and I found the proximity to living nonhuman animals fascinating, if not quite a pleasing olfactory experience, especially with the sow, and (b) there was an active, hand-operated wellwater pump in the backyard, which also fascinated me; I'd seen another of those only at the home of some older relatives in southeast Arkansas. In neither of these cases were limitations of indoor plumbing linked to poverty. My paternal great-uncle in Eudora was a mortician and funeral director whose business extended into north Louisiana and across the river into Mississippi. His brother-in-law, my great-aunt's brother, had been a physician in the same town for many years, and my father grew up facing taunts of "one of them kills 'em, and the other one buries 'em." In what's always seemed to me an odd coincidence, and for reasons I've never been clear about, my maternal grandmother passed a portion of her childhood in little Eudora as well, and she actually had known some of my father's older extended family, including some who were still alive when I was a child.

Over the 1950s my grandparents modernized the house, sold some of the acreage, removed the vestiges of the farm, and created a commodious one- or two-acre getaway for themselves and family. Spending time there became more practical a few months before my tenth birthday when the opening of the Lake Pontchartrain Causeway cut the trip from New Orleans to Covington in half. Until then, the drive required going east of the city to cross the lake via what was known as the 5 Mile Bridge to Slidell on the north shore near the lake's eastern edge and then back west and north to Covington. The nearly twenty-four-mile causeway—the world's longest continuous bridge over water—across the center of the lake cut the hour-long trip to Covington to a half-hour.

I suspect my grandmother, who was an uncommonly strong-willed woman, had had in her mind all along moving to the Covington house upon my grandfather's retirement. He wasn't much of an outdoor hobbyist and found his enjoyment in more urban pursuits like visiting with his old cronies, but she loved the idea of being in the country with the birds she fed and the flowers she cultivated. The house wasn't exactly in the country, really, but it seemed like it. When I was a kid, it may have been just outside the city limits. It was on what was until the late 1960s or 1970s a dirt road and separated by a trickling little creek and large wooded lots on both sides from Covington's equivalent to the "bottoms," a deeply impoverished black area of rude wood houses reminiscent of sharecroppers' shacks and with very limited municipal services. On crossing the creek, the wooded area made the bottoms invisible, and we had next to no contact with its inhabitants. Once in a blue moon on visits, we'd stop in at a little bodega/jook joint to pick up a soda or the like, and I faintly recall rare, fleeting interactions with other children there, though I don't remember seeing any spillover from the bottoms to the sparsely populated area of my grandparents' house, even though they were no more than a quarter mile apart.

When I learned of my grandfather's stroke, I immediately made plans to drive to see him. My grandparents had come to visit us in Atlanta a year earlier, and he made a side trip to Miami to visit his sister and niece who had moved there from Cuba in the mid-1960s. There were signs then that atherosclerosis gave him little lapses in memory; perhaps they would be diagnosed today as transient ischemic attacks, or TIAs. Nevertheless, news of the stroke was gut-wrenching. I was always very close to my maternal grandparents. I was the first grandchild and never felt anything but immensely loved and nurtured by them both. I was definitely the cynosure of my grandfather's eyes. When I was visiting them as a two or three year old, his niece, Ana Mirella, had come to New Orleans for college. She naturally referred to him as "tío." I picked it up from her, and

from there it passed on to all the subsequent grandchildren, as
well as others; he was from then on Tío Macdonald.

My grandparents came to my First Communion in Washington, DC, and attended every other consequential event of
my childhood. I took the train down to spend summers with
them, sometimes alone in a sleeping car under the protective
eyes of a sleeping car porter and with firm instructions not
to leave the train during the long layover in Atlanta. And I
remember their driving me back at the end of the summer,
with the flurry of preparation the day before the drive with
chicken frying and hatboxes lined with napkins and packed
with the food. At the time I had no clue that the relation
between hatboxes stuffed with fried chicken and travel by car
was an accommodation to segregation, which made restaurants
along the way inaccessible. We broke the trip by staying over
in Tuskegee, Alabama, with family friends, the Guzmans, on
the Tuskegee Institute faculty. My grandfather had come to the
United States shortly before World War I to attend Tuskegee
and remained a devoted alumnus all his life; my grandmother
also attended Tuskegee, and, while they knew each other there
vaguely (my grandmother often observed that he ran with a
much faster, more affluent crowd than she had on campus),
they didn't meet formally until he moved to New Orleans after
college. I associated the Guzmans with the husband, Ignacio,
who was an old friend and contemporary of my grandfather
and assumed that the roots of their friendship lay in the Cuba–
Tuskegee connection. (I was not quite correct; Mr. Guzman
was Puerto Rican.) Mrs. Jessie Parkhurst Guzman, I would
realize many years later, was a prominent academic and civil
rights advocate in her own right. I also didn't realize until
years later that the convention of stopping en route to visit the

Guzmans was not merely about spending time with old friends but another accommodation, albeit one available mainly to middle-class travelers, to Jim Crow exclusion from hotels and motels along the way.

My grandfather doted equally on my son as the family's first great-grandchild, and we thought it would be good for him to accompany me on the trip, which was a few weeks before his fourth birthday. When we pulled away from our house that Friday evening, he assured me that he'd keep me awake by talking to me through the long night drive. He was fast asleep by the time we reached the Atlanta airport and slept soundly until we had to exit the uncompleted I-65 about forty miles north of Mobile nearly five hours later. As was my custom on that drive, I refilled the car at the point where I-65 ended, in the Bay Minette/Spanish Fort area. Touré woke up when we left the interstate and made up for the time he'd slept with a torrent of happy, enthusiastic chatter. After gassing up, we headed down the dark, two-lane state highway that would connect with I-10 in Mobile. A mile or two down the road, I began to hear a rattling sound I couldn't place, and the headlights seemed to dim. When I slowed down, the tractor trailer behind us passed, and then I realized that the headlights were so dim I could barely see in front of the car. I pulled off onto the shoulder and turned off the ignition, but the car wouldn't start at all and only made a clicking sound when I turned the key.

I barely had time to be anxious about being stranded on a desolate Alabama roadside when a sheriff's deputy pulled up, perhaps radioed by the trucker. He was courteous and empathetic when I explained what had happened. He offered to drive us to a motel at a nearby town, and he showed us a mechanic's shop, which he said could tow and repair the car in the morning. (After the deputy dropped us off at the motel and we were alone again, Touré said to me, "Daddy, I almost told him to get out of the black community, but I thought I shouldn't." I was pleased at his moral development and reassured by his common sense.) When the car was being towed, the front driver's side wheel fell off. The rattling sound I'd heard was the tire working loose. Apparently, when I'd had the car serviced before leaving Atlanta, the mechanic stripped the lug nuts and compensated by forcing them on with intense pressure. The loss of power we experienced was the result of a dead alternator and, all things considered, was a lucky break. If the alternator hadn't given out, I'd have been driving when the wheel fell off, and that could have been catastrophic. We got the tire repaired. But that was a time when it was still common that suppliers closed on the weekends, and it wasn't possible to obtain an alternator from Mobile on Saturday. We drove the remaining 150 miles or so to New Orleans on a three-hour battery charge and at no more than 50 miles per hour and with no radio.

We got there and replaced the alternator. Everyone with whom we had encounters along the way—the deputy sheriff, motel clerk, the mechanics in the small Alabama town who worked on the car and did the best they could for us—was empathetic, courteous, and respectful. And all were white. Our experience was similar at the auto supply and service business that installed the new alternator, which was a firm my family faithfully patronized, and we received the friendliness and consideration one would expect for familiar customers.

We made our way to the Covington hospital, and my grandfather was so overjoyed at seeing his great-grandson—once my grandmother successfully hectored the duty nurse to permit the child to enter the room—that he held him close and cried. It was a good visit. My grandfather never fully recovered and spent several months in convalescence. He was such a proud, dignified person that I know the idea of being dependent on others for his most intimate functions upset him. He died in mid-January, on my twenty-eighth birthday, a coincidence that has made the date bittersweet ever since.

In the summer of 1974 I worked six weeks in Warren County, North Carolina, on the northeastern border with Virginia, as a field researcher in a project monitoring equity in patterns of local disbursement of federal funds across the region. My graduate fellowship in the political science department at Atlanta University was good and contributed adequately to our household expenses during the academic year, but it didn't extend to summer, when seeking employment in the regular labor market became necessary. During the summer after my first year, I worked two jobs—one at 7-Eleven, in the highest volume store in the city, across from the Bankhead Courts public housing project; the other at a small, federally or foundation-funded business development program, at which my duties consisted of counseling and doing feasibility assessments for aspiring minority entrepreneurs and cleaning the bathrooms. The second summer, because I had become an inadvertent pawn in a tactical power struggle concerning the terms of racial transition in local government, the idea of summer employment outside Atlanta was attractive. I'll explain.

My department chair normally wrote a politics column for the Black History Month edition of an independent local black newspaper, *The Atlanta Voice*. For the 1974 edition, just after Maynard Jackson was inaugurated as the city's first black mayor, the chair was swamped with other commitments and asked whether I'd be up for writing the annual essay. I agreed and tapped out a piece examining the possibilities of and constraints on the newly emerging cohort of black elected officials just before I took off on a recruiting trip for the graduate school. I returned to find that the essay had been well received by the publisher and political editor, and not long afterward I got a call from a woman who had recently moved to the city with a group from the Bay Area to establish an agency dedicated to assisting black farmers and other rural landowners in retaining their land. She called to compliment me on the article and to express shared political sentiments. We met and talked, and I learned that she had been involved in student black radical politics in Berkeley and Oakland, including with the Republic of New Africa, a period-piece of a separatist group whose idea was to agitate for a black plebiscite on establishment of an independent black nation on the current territories of South Carolina, Georgia, Alabama, Mississippi, and Louisiana.

Almost immediately thereafter, the *Voice's* political editor called to inquire whether I'd be interested in writing something on the dramatic recent kidnapping of newspaper heiress Patty Hearst in Berkeley by a shadowy group called the Symbionese Liberation Army. I told him that I didn't know anything at all about the group or the circumstances surrounding the kidnapping but that I had just met a woman from out there who seemed plugged into Bay Area radical politics and that she might be a good person to write something about it. They agreed that she'd do an essay, and she suggested that we collaborate. I demurred, noting that I knew absolutely nothing about California politics, left or otherwise. She insisted that I contribute, and I wrote a framing paragraph for the essay and still suggested there was no reason to add me to the byline and that she could have the paragraph as her own if she liked. I felt a little cheesy about being listed as a co-author of a piece for which I'd done practically nothing. Anyway, the *Voice* published the piece as a news analysis including me as co-author, which I had no problem with apart from the slightly cheesy feeling, and that seemed to be the end of the matter.

Three months later, early on Saturday morning, May 18, I received a phone call from a close neighbor with whom my wife and I had been friendly since he had been her college classmate in New Orleans. He asked whether we'd seen the morning paper yet and, when I indicated we hadn't, he suggested we look because, he said, there's a story about "someone with the same name as you, who was in the same places as you, but it certainly doesn't sound like you." We looked at the morning's edition of the *Atlanta Journal/Constitution* and were stunned to see that beneath the banner headline, "5 SLA Suspects Found Dead In House After Fiery Shootout" and accompanying photos, a headline at the fold read, "Terrorist Fear Put Spy at 'Voice,'" and the first sentence read, "Fear that Atlanta had been infiltrated by hardcore terrorists on the run prompted the planting of an undercover agent in the offices of the Atlanta *Voice*, it was learned Friday." My co-author, who some years later matriculated at Atlanta University and became a prominent political scientist, and I, as well as the historian and distinguished fellow of the Institute of the Black World, Vincent Harding, were fingered as the possible suspects "on the run."

The article was preposterous, irresponsible, and potentially dangerous. It characterized us as "elusive," even though she

worked every day in the office of her agency, and, as my department chair pointed out in an angry letter to the editor of the
Constitution, I was listed in the telephone book, the list of registered voters, and the Fulton County property tax rolls and,
moreover, could be found any day of the week in the political
science department's reading room. The obvious implication
was that the reporter made no attempt at all to reach either of
us and repeated the newspaper's pattern that my chair had long
described as "reporting the black community exclusively from
the police blotter." It was clear that the Atlanta police merely
contacted the FBI and rehearsed whatever garbled information
it passed on. The stigmatization and surveillance were real,
however. For weeks after the article appeared, helicopters flew
in low circles over our house, shining their searchlights over
the property, and we had reason to believe that our phone
was tapped.

What happened was that we were scapegoats in the incumbent police chief's effort to keep his job. The *Voice's* editor and
publisher, J. Lowell Ware, was a gadfly, crusading journalist,
and since the mayoral race the year before had been urging,
even challenging, Maynard Jackson to pledge to fire Chief
John Inman because of the record of police violence and killing
of civilians during his leadership of the department. The mayor
was trying to fire him but faced resistance from some elements
in the business community who either supported Chief Inman
or didn't want Mayor Jackson to make his own appointment.
Inman had obtained an injunction preventing the mayor from
replacing him, and, while the court battle raged, Ware and
the *Voice* kept up the pressure on the mayor to oust him. That
was the context in which Inman surreptitiously placed a black
female undercover cop into the offices of the *Voice;* he was

looking for evidence to incriminate or discredit Ware. Her cover was blown almost immediately, and the mayor declared that "heads would roll" at the police department if Inman couldn't show "sufficient cause" for infiltrating the office. We became the sufficient cause. In addition to the fact that other comparably attractive and desirably remunerative summer jobs were scarce, my family and I decided that my being out of town for a few weeks while the scapegoating hysteria dissipated probably wouldn't be such a bad thing. Moreover, the job's flexibility could facilitate completing my MA thesis. So I headed off to Warren County.

3

"Race" and the New Order Taking Shape within the Old

Warren County was, and remains, sparsely populated; in the mid-1970s its total population was around 16,000. It was majority minority, and that population was apportioned among blacks, who were the county's overall majority, Lumbee Indians, and another, considerably smaller group known as the Haliwa or Haliwa-Saponi Indian tribe. Many of those officially recognized as black in the area were phenotypically indistinguishable from Lumbee and Haliwa-Saponi groups. Contextual and other tacit cues helped inform reasonably accurate guesses as to who was considered what among them. The Haliwa—the name comes from Halifax and Warren, the two counties where the group lives—became known as a distinct identity-group only in the post–World War II decades. I had heard of them since my college years as a population that simply decided no longer to be black and crafted a Native American identity for itself. Friends from the area confirmed that during the late 1940s and 1950s some of their own families split irrevocably over whether to retain their recognized black racial status or pursue Haliwa identity. In 1957 the Haliwa created racially

separate elementary and secondary schools, which the state
and county education agencies recognized, and in 1965 they
successfully petitioned the legislature to recognize the group
name and change designations on its members' birth certifi-
cates from "the colored race" to "the Indian race." The Haliwa
schools did not survive the 1960s because they were racially
segregated and thus violated *Brown* and its legal and institutional implications.

The Haliwa emergence is curious because of its timing.
Consolidation of the binary racial system that undergirded the
southern white supremacist order at the end of the nineteenth
century confronted immigrants previously alien to American
racial ideology with a practical imperative to distance themselves from legal, or customary, classification as black. The
"Delta Chinese," imported initially by planters who imagined
that they would be more tractable than recently emancipated
blacks, are a case in point. Early immigrants located around
and interacted among blacks, which was a natural occurrence
because the populations were slotted into similar roles in the
cotton economy. As the immigrant population stabilized and
settled in, they adjusted to the region's social order. Delta
Chinese came to occupy a classic ethnic middleman merchant's niche and to assert claims to a social and legal position
outside the black/white binary.

The latter effort culminated in *Gong Lum v. Rice,* a 1927 US
Supreme Court case that was the Court's first consideration
of the *Plessy* doctrine's application to public education. Gong
Lum, a Chinese American in Bolivar County, Mississippi, sued
in state court when his daughter was prohibited from attending a white school in the county. The suit did not challenge
the state's right to segregate schools by race but argued instead

that his daughter had been mistakenly classified as "colored." The plaintiff's argument hinged on state of the art (albeit bogus) race theory and sought to demonstrate that Chinese were intermediate between blacks and whites, yet nearer the latter, with respect to both phenotypic characteristics and "civilization." Gong Lum lost the case, but local white elites were sufficiently moved by the argument that they eventually, and quietly, permitted the daughter to attend the white school. Sicilians who arrived later in the nineteenth century, in part to work in Louisiana's cane and cotton fields, and other immigrants also had to navigate the Jim Crow order's Procrustean racial binary and soon enough recognized that, no matter how implausible claims to be white might seem, at a minimum one should strive to be distinguished from blacks.

In a rigidly hierarchical social order like that of the segregationist South, which is based on ascriptive status—that is, status defined by what you supposedly are rather than what you do—the inclination to differentiate oneself from groups consigned to the bottom, while not laudable, is reasonable and understandable. We shouldn't expect heroic action from people who find themselves in oppressive systems. Writing in *The Holocaust in American Life* about the inclination after the fact to judge ordinary Germans harshly for their failure to dissent publicly from the Nazi racialist dictatorship and exterminism, historian Peter Novick flatly rejected the view that how one acts under extreme conditions expresses one's "true" character or commitments.[1] That standard, he argued, predetermines a negative judgment because most people, by definition, will not act heroically under such conditions. They will try to find ways to protect themselves and craft aspirations and self-images that accommodate to the conditions that constrain and threaten them.

The last decades of the nineteenth century and the first decades of the twentieth were the period when the race idea was at its zenith, when "race" had its greatest power in the history of the world, before or since, as a taxonomy for sorting human populations and ranking them hierarchically on the basis of the different qualities, characteristics, and capacities ascribed to them. Nascent American immigration policy established white race as a necessary criterion of eligibility for naturalization as citizens, and immigrants from the Middle and Near East, as well as marginal southern and eastern areas of Europe and its fringes, commonly had to demonstrate their racial suitability. Immigrants' embrace, or pursuit, of white racial classification, therefore, was most of all pragmatically motivated; it was a necessary means to the end of attaining full civic membership in American, and especially southern, society. It did not stem from abstract commitment to white supremacy or hatred of blacks. The American racial binary as the basis for social hierarchy was historically specific and distinctive to American political development. People from elsewhere did not come here steeped in that binary, least of all as the foundation of a social order.

Not only immigrants but groups already here who didn't seem to fit easily within the phenotypic and other characteristics held to define the black/white binary would reasonably respond to the hierarchy's limits by seeking to situate themselves as either outside the binary or, where plausible, as in effect white. In addition to the Delta Chinese, Mexican Americans in Texas, Native Americans, Arabs, and later South Asians commonly strove to distance themselves from identification as black. It was also not unusual for "mixed-race" individuals or groups to assert ascriptive identities outside the racial binary system. Among ostensibly "mixed-race" groups understood to have significant black ancestry are populations anthropologists have classified as "tri-racial isolates" like the Melungeon of the Cumberland Gap region of Appalachia, the Brass Ankles of South Carolina, and the Haliwa and Lumbees of North Carolina.

A cynical perspective on these groups' claims to fall outside the racial binary reduces them ultimately to an objective of spurning identification as black. That view is not entirely without merit, but it is problematic insofar as it implies dishonesty in representation, race disloyalty, or (worse still) self-hatred. Sociologist Brewton Berry found in his classic 1963 study, *Almost White: A Study of Certain Racial Hybrids in the Eastern United States,* that those groups generally denied or greatly diminished the significance of African ancestry.[2] Yet the cynical view is simplistic; it fails to account for the ambiguous and fluid relation between "race" and "culture" and equally fluid and ambiguous notions of "heritage." Even the constructs "racial hybrid" and "tri-racial isolates" treat race as a natural category, an essential marker of human difference rooted in biology. It is possible to be a racial hybrid or tri-racial only if races are real, measurable entities with clear boundaries. Notwithstanding the lucrative scams currently perpetrated under the guise of genetic determinism by both ancestry search firms and the pharmaceutical industry, they are not.

Racial identity is willed or imposed, or both; it has no foundation outside of social experience. Nor, therefore, is racial ancestry or heritage a real thing other than through will or imposition. There are no racial imperatives that demand expression of particular attitudes, behavior, or social practices. Simply put, racial heritage cannot be denied or rejected because there's no such thing as racial heritage. In biological terms, saying "I am black" and saying "I am not black" are equally meaningless statements. Characterizing such groups, then, as denying black racial identity misses the point that, like marginal immigrants, what those groups have sought to reject as a practical matter is being marked as belonging to a population on the bottom of the social order with severely constrained rights and opportunities and social pariah status. It makes sense to view efforts to reject that identification as inauthentic only if we accept the utterly artificial taxonomies of racial classification crafted and imposed in service to enforcing white supremacy.

To be sure, avoiding the consequences of being labeled black has likely played a role in shaping the formulation and evolution of those other indigenous identities, especially as they were publicly asserted, but those populations also can be seen as insisting on notions of groupness at odds with the fictive biology of racial taxonomy and the black/white binary in particular. Indeed, according to her family, Mildred Loving, plaintiff in the landmark 1967 Supreme Court case, *Loving v. Virginia*, was a case in point. The case overturned Virginia's 1924 Racial Integrity Act's prohibition of marriage between "white" and "colored" races, and by extension anti-miscegenation laws generally. Loving attended black schools in Caroline County, Virginia but at the same time considered herself "Indian-Rappahannock," also defined as "colored" under the Virginia law, which mandated the most extensive state program of racial classification the world would see until the Nazis' Nuremberg Laws were enacted just over a decade later. Late in her life Loving reportedly denied having any "black ancestry."

It's not clear whether she meant that she had no known ancestors racially classified as black, none who identified as black, or something else altogether. What is clear is that she was not so much *rejecting* a heritage as *asserting* one. Belief that she was doing the former, that she was in effect "passing" for something that she was not racially, depends on a premise that race marks natural populations, which it does not. One can be "black," as I've indicated, only if that identification is imposed by law or social convention and—especially now, given defeat of the racist Jim Crow order and the changing stakes of racial classification—if one accepts that identification for oneself. As the 2015 contretemps over Rachel Dolezal's representation of herself as black made clear most recently, there are no objective criteria for assigning people to one "race" or another.[3]

It is instructive in this regard that an ironic element in the undoing of early twentieth-century race science was its commitment to producing definitive taxonomies of racial classification. The harder earnest race scientists tried and failed to specify criteria defining and distinguishing "races," the more they exposed the notion's essential incoherence and arbitrariness; their estimates of the number of "basic races" in the world ranged between three and sixty-three.

By the end of the 1960s, race science had been pretty thoroughly debunked in respectable intellectual life, although the folk notions it had sought to validate persisted, with all their ambiguities and essentialist mythology, in organizing most people's everyday perceptions of groups and difference. That is one reason that Mildred Loving's assertion that she had no black ancestry is unclear. Race, culture, ancestry, and heritage all swirl together in popular discourse in what historian of anthropology George Stocking Jr. once described, in

characterizing an early school of race science, as a "vague socio-
biological indeterminism."[4] In the South persistence of folk
racialism mediated transition out of the cultural and ideological premises that anchored the Jim Crow institutional order.
Warren County in the mid-1970s illustrated the simultaneous
continuity of the old and the emergence of the new South,
and not only because of its distinctive population of blacks,
whites, and "tri-racial isolates." When I found myself there in
the midst of that moment, I didn't quite understand the extent
to which the pattern of continuity and change visible there
would foreshadow the postsegregation era's regime of racial
and class power.

My work in the county involved mainly collecting data
from public agencies and interviewing local officials regarding patterns of expenditure of Revenue Sharing and other
federal program funds in connection with enforcement of
anti-discrimination legislation. In Warrenton, the county seat
and my base of operation, government offices were centrally
located in the small downtown square. I decided to use the
local public library, which was located near the square, as a
point for repose and going over my notes and schedule between
appointments as well as for working on my own thesis during
breaks. The first time I entered the library it was empty except
for me and the librarian, who for all the world looked the part
of the small-town southern stereotype. She clearly stereotyped
me as well because after sizing me up with obvious circumspection for about fifteen minutes, she apparently pegged me
as a suspicious outsider, scurried out, and returned a bit later
with the sheriff. (No doubt exacerbating her concern, my hair
was long, and I had a beard.) Luckily, I had interviewed the
sheriff about local expenditure of Law Enforcement Assistance

Administration funds a couple of days earlier, and he reassured her that I posed no threat.

I assume the librarian took me for some sort of "outside militant" agitator. As the sheriff's response suggests, such concern was by that point already a vestige of an earlier time. I don't recall whether either the city or county had any black elected officials yet. It wouldn't have mattered if there had been any, which is one reason I can't recall. A decade after the 1964 Civil Rights Act, which outlawed discrimination in employment and public accommodations, and nearly as long after the 1965 Voting Rights Act, which reenfranchised black Americans in the South, the nature of the social and ideological order through which the regime of ruling class power in the region was reproduced at the everyday level was evolving in concert with the new realities the legislative victories helped create. Of course, folk notions of racial hierarchy and modes of behavior lingered. More than a half-century after the landmark legislation of the 1960s, on a crowded Amtrak business class car I still occasionally muse about Plessy and railcar segregation, which was officially proscribed, at least for interstate travel, by the time I was eight years old.

That lingering power of ideology helps explain how the Haliwa came together as claimants to a new Native American identity only after World War II. Hardly anyone, not even the most hopeful egalitarians, at that point would have imagined that the Jim Crow order would soon be on its last legs. Places like rural Warren County were further removed politically and socially than they were geographically from the urban centers where the Supreme Court's 1944 *Smith v. Allwright* ruling that outlawed exclusionary white primaries led to exponentially increased black voter registration and encouraged the development of a "moderate segregationist" politics that supported enhanced opportunities for blacks within the regime. The judicial and legislative victories did not alter the framework of political and economic subordination that prevailed outside the larger cities. There was civil rights activism in Warren County in the 1960s, but by that time the impetus to assert a distinct Haliwa identity had congealed—reminiscent of the old quip that a sect is a cult with an army and a navy—into a shared commitment to groupness as authentic as any other.

But by the mid-1970s, Haliwa identity had no particular bearing on anything. Black people viewed it with circumspection and a sardonic, mild disdain as an almost comical attempt to escape black racial identification. The breakdown of the Jim Crow order had rendered Haliwa-ness obsolete as a basis for establishing a liminal position within segregation's racial binary. In retrospect, because of a new and discrete intervention, evolving social relations on display then in Warren County both indicated the deeper truth that underlay the white supremacist order and provided a glimpse of what would replace it.

Several years earlier, the county experienced an influx of people and resources associated with Floyd McKissick's Soul City project. McKissick, who as a student had desegregated the University of North Carolina Law School, had been a civil rights attorney and activist and national director of the Congress of Racial Equality. He also harbored a dream of developing a new black city in the area. A 1970 grant from the US Department of Housing and Urban Development (HUD), through the Urban Growth and New Community Development Act, launched McKissick's enterprise. I was familiar with the project and had assisted in a shopping habits and patterns study associated with it at the agency where I worked in Durham before leaving to attend graduate school. McKissick assembled a staff of up to sixty or so professionals who worked for Soul City on site in Warren County. At one point or another their ranks included Eva Clayton, who later would spend a decade on the Warren County Commission and another decade in Congress, and Harvey Gantt, who had been the first black student to attend Clemson University, earned an advanced degree in architecture from MIT, and later was two-term mayor of Charlotte and two-time Democratic nominee for the US Senate. A former co-worker of mine in Durham, a certified public accountant, worked there for a time as well. Coincident with his support of President Nixon's reelection, in 1972 McKissick received another HUD grant of $14 million for Soul City. But nothing much ever came of the project on its own terms; it's worth mentioning here mainly because of the light that its presence shed on how southern elites could adapt to the end of Jim Crow.

I spent most of my work time in Warrenton in public agencies and interacting with public officials and functionaries. I didn't know what to expect from those interactions when I got there and was reassured to find that, even when my interlocutors seemed initially quizzical or stand-offish, they were typically responsive, and, in that southern way, cordial and even friendly. Most of all, they responded to me as a peer. At the same time, that vantage point afforded ample opportunity to observe their interactions with other blacks and Indians or "tri-racial isolates." (Many whites took the liminal status claims of the latter groups with a grain of salt, to say the least. Instructively, Virginia's Racial Integrity Law classified Indians

as "colored" in part because its author, Walter A. Plecker, registrar of the state's Bureau of Vital Statistics and a militant
white supremacist and eugenicist, believed that most of the
state's Indian population had African antecedents and were
attempting to pass to avoid segregation. The law did include
a "Pocahontas" exception as an escape clause for those among
the state's hereditary upper-class First Families of Virginia,
who claimed descent from the legendary Powhatan woman.
Plecker and his mentor, Madison Grant, the Charles Murray
of his day, joked cynically that the exception most likely permitted some with African ancestry to slip through as white but
agreed that that was an acceptable price to pay for being able to
pass the legislation.) The difference was striking. The standard
engagement with locals was governed by the familiar dynamic
of paternalism and deference, and the shift was automatic and
instantaneous, like code-switching.

And it wasn't about me. Blacks associated with Soul City
received the same treatment as I. If anything, their presence
sanitized mine, even overriding my beard and long hair. At
first, I thought the basis for the difference was a distinction
between locals and outsiders, as the changes over the previous
decade had encouraged greater sensitivity to recognizing those
likely to squawk and bring outside pressure and those not.
Still, if it hadn't been for the Soul City contingent, I suspect I'd
have drawn more skepticism as a lone outsider. On reflection,
I realized that the distinction had a more complex foundation.
Soul City brought federal resources into the county. During
my time there, for example, the enterprise was responsible for
funding or securing funding for a new water system for Warren
and an adjacent county. Soul City personnel earned far more
than locals, and even though many in effect commuted from

Durham, they still pumped money into the local economy, and the institution spent, or promised to spend, far more.

Whether those white elites' dealings with upper status black outsiders or lower status locals were more genuine can't be known and in any case is irrelevant. Motives are often complex, and, as my father often observed, sincerity is vastly overrated as a virtue. The significant point is that the changing conditions generating and attendant to the defeat of the Jim Crow order provided incentives for changed behavior. (Illustratively, and comically, the day after Lyndon Johnson signed the 1964 Civil Rights Act, the white barber in tiny Eudora walked down the street to my Great-Uncle Clarence's funeral home to announce, "Mr. Bethune, now that the law has changed, I'd certainly appreciate your business.") That's why, following Novick's observation about the folly of such abstract moral judgments, analyses of the past (or present for that matter) that hinge on uncovering deep commitments to racism or white supremacy don't help us understand anything.

In the summer of 1974, as I've noted, Maynard Jackson was well into the first year of his first term as Atlanta's mayor, with black majorities on both the City Council and school board, and Andrew Young was completing his first term as the first black congressman elected from the South in the twentieth century. Nearer to Warren County, Howard Lee was in his third two-year term as the first black mayor of Chapel Hill, and Charles Lightner was mayor of Raleigh. In North Carolina, as in big cities across the South, federal War on Poverty, Great Society, and Model Cities spending had encouraged black incorporation into local governing coalitions, policy-making, and administration. Soul City accelerated that process in Warren County in contrast to other rural areas in the region.

Melissa Fay Greene, in her wonderful and poignant book, *Praying for Sheetrock,* explores the longer and more fraught path of change in rural McIntosh County, Georgia.[5]

In part because of its unusual racial composition but mainly because of the impact of Soul City's presence, that moment in Warren County condensed in a particularly clear way a reality that white supremacist ideology was always meant to conceal. While the Jim Crow order was explicitly and definitively about race, at the same time it was fundamentally not really about race at all. What at first blush appeared to be white elites' distinction between black locals and outsiders was a class distinction. And it wasn't simply a distinction between classes of black people who could make trouble and those who couldn't. Black professionals shared a perspective and worldview with their white counterparts, one that had to do with the premises of governance and the protocols of management and administration as well as middle-class lifestyle.

It's probable that the whites continued to harbor racialist stereotypes about blacks generically, including the black class peers with whom they interacted. Old habits die hard, and folk knowledge—what we know because we know it—can be impervious to contradiction by study and experience. But that likelihood doesn't negate the significance of the interracial class dynamic that governed interactions between white elites and, respectively, their nonwhite class peers and perceived inferiors. No matter what may have been in their "hearts," Warren County officials were able to accept and deal with black class peers as equals and with other blacks in ways continuous with the old order.

One takeaway from that dynamic is that static notions like "race relations" (a concept that originated with Booker T.

Washington's program of accommodation to white supremacy, it should be recalled) don't help us understand, and may even obscure, the Jim Crow order and what emerged out of its defeat. If whites' commitments to racism or white supremacy produce such radically different practical expressions, then we have to question how much such commitments really explain. Similarly, if we accept that "race" has no biological foundation and is a fluid, contextual, and historically contingent notion, and if we consider the social and ideological work that notion does, then class distinctions among blacks like those Warren County elites displayed are in effect also *racial* distinctions in the sense that they attach sharply different social meanings and consequences to being "black" in ways that wouldn't have been possible within the Jim Crow order grounded on the generic black/white binary.

In order words, the victories of the 1960s, while not ushering in a "colorblind" society, did provide space for making racelike distinctions within populations already defined by race. Thus, just as in the heyday of early twentieth-century race science, the "white" population was held to include many different "subraces," each with its own supposed racial characteristics, elimination of a social and political order based explicitly on the black/white binary as a legally enforced limit on rights, status and aspirations enabled a commonsense expression of racelike distinctions among blacks. I have argued for some time that assertion of the existence of an "urban underclass," which gained currency over the 1980s to signal a distinct population imagined to be bounded by specific group characteristics, was, for all intents and purposes, a call for recognizing such a subrace.

To return to the curious case of the Haliwa, what gave their effort to escape the black/white binary its rather pathetic quality is not that it was an attempt to deny "black heritage" but that it couldn't foresee the racialist order's instability in the postwar decades and assumed that operating within its precepts could be more advantageous than would turn out to be correct. By the time the group attained official recognition as a racially distinct population, the order already had begun to break down, as the fate of the Haliwa schools demonstrated. With respect to group status, by the mid-1970s the Haliwa label was no more than an idiosyncratic modifier on a subordinate position defined by class dynamics within the local political economy; at most, it is a small node in the post-segregation era's orrery of celebratory ethnicity.

4

The New Order and the Obsolescence of "Passing"

The changing significance of such liminal identities in a context in which racial classification no longer has the determinative force that it once did also suggests a perspective on the somewhat related phenomenon of racial "passing." The notion typically refers to individual efforts to reject black identification through falsely claiming some nonblack racial identity that could provide a gateway to greater opportunity and higher social standing. St. Clair Drake and Horace Cayton, Jr. give the practice a clear-eyed and well-grounded treatment in all its variety and ramifications in their classic 1945 Chicago case study, *Black Metropolis: A Study of Negro Life in a Northern City*.[1] The phenomenon has engaged literary imagination since the nineteenth century; novelists Nella Larsen, Jessie Fauset, James Weldon Johnson, William Faulkner, Philip Roth, Ralph Ellison, and even Mark Twain have explored the theme in various ways. In turn-of-the-twentieth century romances of racial uplift (for example, in novels by Frances Harper and Sutton Griggs), passing often appeared as a road not taken, evidence of the nobility of character of some man or woman who could have "crossed over" successfully but chose not to out of race loyalty and commitment to some program of race advancement.

Passing has been represented dramatically in tragic or naturalistic terms, with the implication that attempts to escape from what one "really is" inevitably come a cropper. Often it has been treated as indicating a character flaw or moral defect, similar to the figure of the tragic mulatto supposedly afflicted by wanting to aspire beyond blacks' natural station or to reject one's heritage out of something akin to self-hatred. Disparagement of passing as an aspiration beyond one's natural place is a judgment that affirms the legitimacy of racial hierarchy. Thus, D. W. Griffith's 1915 *Birth of a Nation,* the white supremacist porno glorifying the Ku Klux Klan, depicted "mulattoes" as skulking and devious, congenital malcontents (all played by tanned-up white actors) driven by resentment at their inability to be white. In 1942, seven years after enactment of the Nuremberg Laws, Walter Plecker sought to tighten enforcement of Virginia's Racial Integrity Law to counter "the determined effort to escape from the negro [sic] race of groups of 'free issues,' or descendants of 'free mulattoes' of early days, so listed prior to 1865 … as distinguished from slave negroes."[2] Plecker feared that the "Indian" loophole would assist such "mongrels" in "making a rush to register as white,"[3] and he reminded county registrars that, under the law, attempting to perpetrate such a "fraud" carried a sentence of one year in the penitentiary.

Some seemingly more sympathetic portrayals focused on the tragedy and torment of individuals' attempts to pass and their feeling caught between their actual or official and aspirational identities. The two versions of the film *Imitation of*

Life, in 1934 and 1959, exemplified this characterization. These and other segregation-era popular cultural treatments of passing, such as the 1960 film, *I Passed for White,* while not overtly judgmental like Griffith's, accommodated to a notion of natural and fundamental racial difference that lives within the individual despite outward appearances. The later films obscured that premise by embodying the racial essence in the passer's relatives, particularly long-suffering and rejected black mothers. That convention fit the postwar retreat from early twentieth-century convictions that race was marked by hard biological difference and could even underscore the earlier view's folly. Yet it reflected the vaguer notions of difference that hovered between biology and culture, which were condensed in notions of "heritage." Personalizing essential difference in the figure of rejected family members finessed the issue by constructing passing as a moral or psychological dilemma. Lurking beneath, however, was a naturalizing premise reminiscent of philosopher Horace Kallen's expressly racialist contention that cultural heritage is indelible because you "cannot change your grandfather."[4]

Objection to passing as a rejection of one's heritage also implies an obligation of group loyalty. That's the other side of the coin of those Victorian race romances that laud the nobility of characters who actively choose to acknowledge themselves as black and embrace efforts to challenge the hierarchy or at least improve blacks' prospects within it. But that view, no less than Griffith's, Plecker's, and the others', presumes that racial classification defines what one "really" is, even though Plecker's anxiety indicates the race idea's fundamental fluidity and insubstantiality, how thoroughly its roots lie in a particular technology of social, political, and economic hierarchy. In fact, apart from that specific technology of hierarchy and the social order of which it was an instrument, passing as a phenomenon loses much, if not all, of its social meaning.

In New Orleans and elsewhere in the phenotypic gumbo of south Louisiana, passing was familiar enough to be part of colloquial experience. It generated its own social category, the *passant blanc*. In the 1960 gubernatorial race, when asked by a reporter how he intended to appeal to the white vote in south Louisiana, candidate Earl K. Long, the legendary Huey P.'s brother, remarked that it was possible to feed all the truly white people in south Louisiana off one plate of red beans and rice.

Under the Jim Crow order, in fact, passing was often a straightforwardly pragmatic phenomenon, unburdened by the stuff of the overwrought morality play rehearsed in films, literature, and the ruminations of race-conscious commentators of all sorts.

My first encounter with passing as a phenomenon had come in that context, when I was a child visiting my grandparents. A family friend from my mother's generation stopped by to visit on her occasional trips "home" from what appeared to be a rather glamorous life in California. She stayed at elegant, whites-only hotels downtown from whence she would make not quite surreptitious sorties to visit old friends and family. I understood from overhearing adults' banter that she was "passing for white" in California, a circumstance that she seemed to discuss freely and expected that others took in stride as well. As a teen in the early 1960s, I knew an extended family in the city's Seventh Ward who occupied the two sides of a duplex house. The respective household heads were first cousins with the same surname and, as I recall, looked very much alike. The family on one side lived as black; that on the other side lived as white, and they all acknowledged one another. I also learned some years after I graduated that a couple of my old high school buddies had moved out West and become white, and one had compounded the transition by coming out as gay.

Among black people, speculation about detecting possible *passant blanc* strangers could be a running joke or even something like casual sport. I confess that to this day I occasionally muse, out of habit yet in full awareness of the folly of the race idea, whether some random person I encounter out and about really believes himself or herself to be white. While waiting to board a flight to New Orleans a few months before writing this, I noticed from her boarding pass that the presumably white, middle-aged passenger queued immediately in front of me had the same distinctive French surname as my high school girlfriend. In an impish gesture, whose impishness would be comprehensible only within the fundamentally pathological normative order of Jim Crow and its racial etiquette, I mentioned that fact to her. A half-century earlier, or even less, that observation would have been a provocation, possibly a serious one, as it would've implied that either my ex-girlfriend was white or my fellow passenger wasn't. Instead, she showed no sign of affront and mentioned that she often receives calls and mail intended for others with the surname, including flowers meant for one with a given name close to hers.

Among blacks the trope of spotting the passer also underwrote a genre of urban legend that made its own ironic critique of white supremacist ideology, namely, rumors that well-known white supremacists were themselves *passant blanc*. Some particularly striking illustrations remain fresh in my mind from the early 1960s.

In 1962, the Catholic Archbishop excommunicated three notorious white supremacists, including Jackson Ricau, head of the local chapter of the infamous Citizens Council, for their efforts to incite rebellion against the Archdiocese's decision to desegregate its parochial schools. The other two were, if anything, more prominent avatars of white supremacist activism than Ricau. Leander Perez had long been considered one of the most vicious segregationists in the state from the perch of his old-school political fiefdom in nearby Plaquemines Parish. The third of the group, Una Gaillot, had made her mark among segregationist militants as the Madame Defarge of the white opposition during the 1960–61 public school desegregation crisis and later appealed without success to President Johnson to secure her son's re-assignment to an all-white Marine Corps unit. Later still, she attempted (also unsuccessfully) to sue the US government because of the Department of Health, Education, and Welfare's policy of denying funds to state hospitals that continued to classify blood according to the donor's race; her aim was to prevent the possibility that she might in the future receive blood from "nonwhite" donors.

I never heard anything regarding Ricau, which doesn't mean that there were no such rumors about him; an effect of hypodescent—the "one-drop rule"—was that one could appear as emphatically and unambiguously white as models in a Nazi racial hygiene magazine and still not be so officially, and the phenotypic standards for qualifying as white were less demanding in south Louisiana than elsewhere in the country. (I occasionally show students a photo, taken at the end of the 1980s, of the New Orleans mayors then living and ask them to identify on the spot which, if any, of the four were black. Two were, but no one can pick them out with confidence without cheating.) Word did circulate in my networks, though, about both Perez and Gaillot. During her emergence in the school desegregation fight, I heard from various quarters that she had attended the same black Catholic high school as my mother, her siblings, and I and that she married white to live in the Iberville Housing Project, which at that point was reserved for white occupancy. The story followed the pattern of the urban legend: those who retailed it didn't claim firsthand knowledge of her past themselves but reported knowing someone who knew someone who knew her. The Gaillot story didn't merely imply (as was common to the tale type) that her extreme racial animus was defensive, a twisted attempt to cover her tracks; it suggested another layer of pathology as well. Our high school, albeit segregated, was generally considered an elite institution, and the public housing projects, without regard to their occupants' race, were already being stigmatized in class terms. So this wrinkle of the Gaillot story suggested that she'd rather be lower class white than middle-class or respectable black. The Perez story, or at least the version I knew, was less widely circulated. The word was that he was a relative of my first wife's grandmother. I suspect that she wasn't the only black grandmother purported to have a family connection to him.

In the Jim Crow environment, it was clear that passing was often instrumental. For instance, for a couple of years when I was in high school, a man wearing a tie and short-sleeved shirt with a pen in a pocket protector boarded the bus on my route to school every morning at the intersection of Tulane and Carrollton Avenues and rode about twenty minutes to the intersection of Louisiana and St. Charles Avenues, seemingly on the way to work. He sat stiffly in the long seat just behind the driver and blanched in anxiety, visibly gripping the pole, at every stop along the way when new passengers boarded. The black cognoscenti on the bus suspected that he was passing to hold a job for which he probably would not have been eligible if he were recognized as black, and his daily bus ride was stalked by the possibility that some black person he knew would recognize him and blow his cover. (Once, on the bus returning from school, I encountered the *passant blanc*'s equal and opposite number. A middle-aged woman one would never assume to be anything other than white sat alone toward the very back of the not-at-all-crowded bus—which meant that she chose to sit in a section of the bus where blacks normally sat—and held forth, talking to no one in particular, on the iniquities and hypocrisies of white people. As I recall, her bill of particulars centered on white men's sexual predation on black women, and she referred to her phenotypic appearance as evidence of the crimes, noting that there was no other way she could look like she did. Who knows what the woman's "actual" story was, whether she was officially black or not. Obviously, she was tortured in some way that overlapped, or at least expressed itself in relation to, the perverse and irrational, and profoundly unjust, system of racial regulation. It also may be worth pointing out that I hadn't thought of this incident in the context of the passing issue until I recently watched a clip of an interview with white antiracist guru Robin DiAngelo, and a friend remarked that she could be a *passant blanc* herself.)

Passing also could be purely frivolous. In her final instructions for our field trip to the train station to examine its 120-foot-long mural depicting the history of New Orleans and Louisiana, our ninth-grade civics teacher gave us an admonition that struck me even then as at odds with what our lessons praised as the wonders of American democracy. The teacher, who came from a well-known Baton Rouge Creole family, cautioned us that, while "some of you might be able to use whichever restrooms and lunch counters you choose," it was important to refrain from doing so and to obey the law. She never mentioned segregation, but she didn't have to. Everyone knew what she meant. And everyone also knew that the admonition was directed toward the considerable number of our classmates who, because of phenotypic appearance, could pass plausibly. Her concern wasn't that any of those students would try to use the field trip to escape from black identity through some wormhole in the terminal or to express politically articulate dissent from Jim Crow laws. The danger she perceived was the adolescent impulse to get away with flouting law and convention. She wanted to nip in the bud the temptation to use whites-only restrooms or lunch counters as a vehicle for indulging that impulse. The field trip went off without a hitch, even though a few students playfully threatened to transgress.

That new, modern train station terminal had opened only a few years before. I knew it pretty well as a kid, both from having ridden the train on summer trips down there and because of the very tasty hamburgers served in the lunch counter café. After Mass on Sunday morning, my grandparents went either to the French Market to buy fruit and produce off the trucks or to McKenzie's or Gambino's bakery for breads and some pastries, including maybe an éclair or two for me. (I never figured out what led them to go to one or the other on a given Sunday, though I faintly recall that Gambino's was a bit more luxurious in the pastry department.) The train station joined the rotation of pleasant post-Mass diversions probably not too long after it opened, which suited me fine because of the hamburgers. I recall as well that the station in its early days was basically across the street from the black-owned Patterson Hotel in a small, somewhat rundown black business and residential district. Seeing a multistory hotel with black people all around it in a largely black area made an impression on me. It wasn't mind-blowing; I'd seen Harlem and U Street. It just stuck in my mind.

The hotel and commercial district weren't around much longer in any case. The new train station was an element of a larger Public Improvement Project that included construction of a downtown expressway and an associated overpass and on and off ramps, all of which spelled the end of that utterly forgotten location, recalled now as the generically dilapidated area cleared to make way for the terminal and other improvements. Unsurprisingly, neither the city government nor the Housing Authority of New Orleans made efforts to relocate residents who were displaced.

Although I recall the Patterson Hotel across the street and the appeal of the mural inside, I have no recollection of noting that the terminal's restrooms and lunch counters were racially separate until that field trip several years later. Perhaps that was because they weren't signposted as such. I suspect my enthusiasm for the hamburgers overwhelmed my awareness that the lunch counter was Jim Crow. I know that in those earlier years I was so taken with the strawberry ice cream soda served at the McCrory's Five and Dime store on Canal Street—a few years later, along with the F. W. Woolworth's also on Canal, a principal target of sit-ins—that the fact that it was available only at a Jim Crow lunch counter hardly registered with me.

Pursuit of such special delicacies could provoke transgression of the rules of petty apartheid as well as acquiescence to them. This is yet another way that passing could be trivially instrumental and utterly fleeting—that is, without any larger meaning at all. Into the 1960s one of the two best-known French Quarter beignet and coffee shops didn't permit blacks to enter the store to make take-out orders. I don't recall the other establishment's racial practices; I assume they must have been similar, but, as with department stores and other commercial establishments, there could be idiosyncratic variations in the etiquette of enforcing segregation. Occasionally, my family would develop a collective hankering for fresh beignets, and the most efficient (or least objectionable, or maybe the only; I no longer recall) way to obtain them was through circumventing the racial regulation. That project required hectoring my grandmother, one of the few in the family who could pull it off easily, to go inside and conduct the transaction. She would do so eventually under protest, kvetching all the way into the store and back to the car. The other family member most capable of pulling off the mission smoothly was an aunt who lived "away," as New Orleanians commonly say. When she visited, her legendary sweet tooth made her a less resistant minion of our desires than my grandmother. In any event, we all appreciated their willingness to take one for the team.

Neither my grandmother nor her expatriate daughter experienced any existential anxiety, not even a speed bump, in momentarily passing to get a box of beignets. To be sure, both were irked by the injustice and irrationality of the racial order that made deception necessary for even so trivial an act, but neither considered for an instant that perpetrating that deception reflected at all on her values or identity. It was an instrumental act, even if perhaps a rather distasteful one. More recently, my mother related another instance of my grandmother's passing that underscores its banal instrumentality.

In the late 1930s or 1940s, the etiquette of enforcing segregation in New Orleans's public transit called for blacks to queue up after whites to board streetcars. My grandmother, who worked as a seamstress during the Depression, on her way home from work one day lined up with the whites, but, when she boarded, she walked back behind the movable "For Colored Patrons Only" sign to take her seat. I don't know whether she joined the whites-only boarding because it was raining, she was tired or hot, simply didn't feel like waiting, or felt ornery. Her open transgression provoked a (presumably) legally white woman to march back to her seat to chastise her, which in turn prompted my grandmother to tell the woman off. My grandmother had a well-deserved reputation for feistiness, but it was the anonymity of the big city that enabled her to transgress racial etiquette so brazenly with no repercussion other than being scolded by a busybody and, especially, to tell off the busybody with impunity. This speaks to New Orleans's reputation for relative laxity in enforcement of racial regulation. For example, both whites and blacks locally had opposed enforcement of the state's 1902 law mandating racial segregation in municipal transit as an unnecessary inconvenience. Local transit companies also opposed it on financial grounds.

My grandmother's transgression of racial etiquette also provides an important counternarrative to the voluntarist myth of Rosa Parks as a seamstress who simply one day felt too tired to give up her seat on the Montgomery bus to a white patron. By now, most people must know that Parks was an officer in the local NAACP chapter, had been trained as an organizer at the famed Highlander Folk School in Tennessee, and had been carefully selected by the Montgomery Improvement Association to be the test case for the challenge to segregation. Because Elizabeth "Bessie" Collins Macdonald's breach of racial etiquette actually *was* a spontaneous act of individual defiance, no one outside our family knows anything about it. And it was not boarding with the whites, which was surreptitious, as passing is by definition, that made her defiance open, but taking a seat in the car's black section. We can be certain as well that she was not the only black person to engage in such acts of spontaneous open defiance in New Orleans or elsewhere. They are unknown because their defiance was spontaneous and individual and therefore had no impact on anything.

So south Louisiana generally and New Orleans in particular provided a special lens onto passing as a phenomenon. Both whimsical passing for beignets or to shorten time in a streetcar line and strategic passing for access to better jobs or housing typically were most often instrumental and without the existential rumination and angst depicted in novels and films. Nevertheless, among black people, especially those who embraced a politicized race consciousness, even whimsical passing could be seen as violating a norm of solidarity based on commonality of racial condition. From that perspective, any sort of passing could amount to an attempt to elude strictures imposed on blacks as blacks by in effect submerging, if not openly denying, black racial identity.

That issue rose to the fore during the moment of racial transition in local politics in the 1970s and 1980s, when an exuberant racial populism reinforced a discourse centered on authenticity—being "really black" in commitments, character, and aspirations—as a criterion of political legitimacy. In the 1986 New Orleans mayoral runoff election, the first featuring

two black candidates and a black majority voting-age population, some anonymous supporters of state senator and future
congressman William Jefferson circulated flyers alleging that his
opponent, City Councilor Sidney Barthelemy, had routinely
passed for white in the 1960s in order to patronize segregated French Quarter clubs and restaurants. The intent was to
impugn Barthelemy's race loyalty and character. The tactic may
have had some impact; Jefferson garnered 70 percent of blacks'
votes, but Barthelemy was elected with 58 percent of the vote
overall, including 86 percent support from white voters. In his
successful bid for re-election in 1990, running against a white
challenger, black voters seemed to accept Barthelemy's racial
bona fides. He received 86 percent of blacks' votes and only
23 percent of whites'.

Instructively, the Jefferson camp's charge was that Barthelemy
had occasionally passed during the segregation era, not more
recently. Passing as social practice was inseparable from the Jim
Crow regime of racial regulation. Instrumental passing was
rendered obsolete by the demise of the segregationist order.
Random individuals certainly still attempt to work out idiosyncratic issues bearing on race and identity by exchanging one
racial identification for another, but the victories of the 1960s
made it no longer necessary to undertake even momentary
racial subterfuge to gain access to decent jobs or engage in con-
sumption of goods and services on a basis unimpeded by race.

Ralph Ellison once remarked that blacks could spot the
passant blanc because it was difficult for them to affect the
presumptive sense of easy mastery that whites were born to
and raised with. Ellison was astute in naming what, in addition
to our heightened awareness of little phenotypic ambiguities,
gave passers away to us. Black people were particularly sensitive

to the tacit markers of having been socialized into subordination, such as the reflex to drop one's eyes in the presence of a strange white person; they had to be in order to perform submissiveness automatically. That's how, for example, we could recognize as a *passant blanc* (or believed we could anyway) the beleaguered fellow whose bus ride to work was fraught with anxiety over being exposed. However, just how much that seemingly preternatural ability to detect passers hinged on the cultural codes of the Jim Crow order would be brought home to me decades later.

In the mid-1990s, my good friend Joe Wood, then a young, very talented *Village Voice* editor who would disappear tragically at the end of the century while birdwatching on Mt. Rainier, was intrigued by the Louisiana Creole population in relation to his project exploring the vagaries of race and identity. I had a conference to attend in New Orleans and agreed to meet him there for the Jazz & Heritage Festival to serve as something like a native guide. After several hours on the Fair Grounds at Jazz Fest, I realized that among the potpourri of more or less swarthy attendees it was no longer possible for me even to speculate on who was considered to be what racially. People who may have identified as Cubans and Hondurans, South Asians, Italian (largely Sicilian) Americans, Isleños from the Canary Islands, and other nominal whites formed a physically and behaviorally indistinguishable blur with whoever may have been (black) Creoles. That was especially the case among the middle-class young people who'd come of age after Jim Crow. No matter what they may have presumed themselves or appeared to others to be, or however they'd been classified by the state, the absence of tacit cues that might have helped to draw even purely speculative racial lines through so much of the crowd threw into relief just how much "passing" was an artifact of the segregationist order. Explicit subordination along racial lines obscured the fact that the sense of mastery that Ellison noted was a reflection of class position as well as racial status. Thirty years after the victories of the civil rights movement, blacks and other nonwhites had long since gained access to that realm of presumptive mastery; passing lost its material foundation and persists only as a product of individual quirk of character or an object of romantic fascination about the past.

5

Echoes, Scar Tissue, and Historicity

In the summer of 1993 I drove with my son to Chicago from New Orleans, where he'd just finished a year after college working temporary jobs, most memorably in the Complaints Department of the Orleans Parish Sewerage and Water Board. He was preparing to enter graduate school in the fall. On our way out of town we stopped to say goodbye to my then ninety-six-year-old grandmother and shared an impromptu encounter with the singer, Little Richard. While driving past, he had noticed the nursing home where she spent her last few years, which was operated by an order of black nuns, and he pulled off the road to visit with its residents. The double blast from the past of Little Richard and conversation with my grandmother turned out to be an apt beginning for our trip.

After driving a few hours in Mississippi, we left the interstate highway near Vicksburg and drove through northeast Louisiana on US 65 to see relatives in Eudora. This was the old route that my parents and I had taken on car trips from Pine Bluff to New Orleans when I was a kid and my first time on this stretch of it since then.

My parents and I always left Pine Bluff in the wee hours of the morning. The first stopping point was in Louisiana, at Tallulah, in Madison Parish. They were particularly anxious driving through north Louisiana's river parishes, through towns like Waterproof and Ferriday—home of televangelist Jimmy Swaggart and his cousin, the rock and roll legend Jerry Lee Lewis, and just a bit upriver from Natchez, Mississippi, home to their other cousin, country and western night club impresario Mickey Gilley. Those small, Black Belt cities on the Mississippi had reputations for being among the most treacherous hotbeds of white supremacist militance. John Barry, in his magisterial social history of the region, *Rising Tide: The Great Mississippi Flood of 1927 and How It Changed America,* reports that between 1889 and 1927 demographically similar Morehouse Parish, an hour away from Tallulah, had more lynchings per capita than any other county in the United States.[1]

Tallulah had a small black-owned hotel and restaurant, where I'd beg my parents for hamburgers. (My love for hamburgers was so great that my dad sometimes called me Wimpy after the Popeye cartoon character whose tag line was "I'll gladly pay you Tuesday for a hamburger today.") They always displayed mixed emotions about stopping at the Tallulah establishment. They welcomed a break from the road, but as was frequently the situation with restaurants accompanied by hotels, the place may have had a sometimes rowdy or even more questionable clientele. That reservation no doubt added to their general anxiety about stopping in those river towns. When I spent a day in Tallulah later in the mid-1990s, I found the still pretty much intact ruins of the building that had housed the hotel-restaurant. It had been a very modest place indeed, and, looking back from the sight of the building, I could sense the basis for my parents' hesitation.

I remember on one of those trips seeing my first chain motel —a Holiday Inn or Albert Pick—in either Vidalia, Louisiana, or Vicksburg, Mississippi, and asking to stop. I think I must not have gotten my hamburger in Tallulah or just greedily wanted another or possibly was taken by the idea of staying in a motel. I was still confused enough about the Jim Crow world's boundaries that I had some difficulty understanding why the motel was off-limits. As the reason settled in on me, it crystallized a hatred that persisted for more than a decade.

In addition to the possibility of a hamburger in Tallulah, the drive had two other highlights. One was the roadside reptile farm in LaPlace, Louisiana, between Baton Rouge and New Orleans. I badgered my father on every trip to stop and let me go in. He finally relented, but when I got out of our car in the dirt parking lot, I saw that the ground was filled with suspicious-looking holes. I expressed concern that they might be snake holes but wasn't much relieved when my father informed me that they housed rodents that were fed to the snakes. I'd seen snakes swallowing pigs and the like on television—even a python that wrapped itself around a tiger driven by hunger to launch a foolhardy attack. But I wasn't quite ready for the ugly reality of rabbits and chipmunks being fed live to them. Then, the first sight we saw on walking through the entrance was a young woman at the ticket turnstile with a large constrictor wrapped around her. No cage, no glass—just a live, writhing, huge snake. And I was supposed to walk right next to it to get into the reptile farm's main rooms. That was too much. I instantly turned and ran out and was well on my way back to our car, tiptoeing around the many holes in the ground. (I'd displayed that hair-trigger reflex for self-preservation a half-dozen years earlier. We frequented the old Laff Movie theater in New York—I was a big fan of the Bowery Boys and Francis the Talking Mule. On one occasion we saw a 3D Abbott and Costello film, I believe, that opened with a fierce gorilla leaping out of the screen. I was seated next to the aisle, and my father barely caught up to me in the lobby before I made it outside.) At the snake farm, however, my father followed me outside and insisted that I return. I'd badgered and begged for too long. His revenge was to force me to get what I'd been asking for. Needless to say, I made no subsequent requests to pull off the highway at LaPlace. Some months later, the young woman, the proprietor's teenage niece, met a tragic death from a cobra bite. Serum made from the blood of Marlon Perkins, the famous naturalist, was flown in by navy jet from Pensacola but arrived too late to save her.

The other point of excitement on the long ride was a place where I prayed we'd never stop, a small Louisiana hamlet called Transylvania, in East Carroll Parish near Lake Providence in the extreme northeastern corner of the state. The name mesmerized me and filled me with horror. With such a name, vampires must have been around. In the late 1950s there was hardly anything to be seen on driving past Transylvania except a steepled, brick church and a few small, dispersed houses. We usually drove through before dawn, which made the town seem all the more mysterious; I never saw any life in the area. I had a classic child's love–hate relationship with Transylvania. I was disappointed whenever I slept through it but when awake I inevitably managed to work myself into a lather of fear that, if nothing else, broke the trip's boredom. The town,

I later learned, was named in the antebellum era by a large landowner in honor of his alma mater, Transylvania University, in Kentucky.

On the drive with my son in the 1990s, I was intrigued to learn that Transylvania's local elites in the three decades and a half since my last visit had decided to try to capitalize on the little hamlet's one distinguishing feature. As we approached, from a few miles away we saw the water tower, bearing the town's name and sporting huge painted black bat wings. We stopped for gas at a roadside service station with a large general store. Nearly a third of the store's inventory was vampire and bat kitsch—masks and other paraphernalia and cheap ceramic figurines. There were rows of Draculas of many sorts. There were almost as many rows of assorted mammy and "coon" figures in yet greater variety.

When we gassed up the car, we chatted for several minutes with the genial attendant, a young black man about my son's age. He was curious about our destination and point of departure. He was demonstrably excited to hear that we were going from New Orleans to Chicago. He'd never been to either place, hardly had ventured from his little node of the Mississippi Delta region, with its bat kitsch, scaled-back cotton economy, and white supremacist nostalgia. The two cities' names carried a magical air for him, and he was delighted to have vicarious contact with them through us, especially my son, who was his peer. His reaction was poignant because it reflected how narrow his actual world was. Not narrow in the sense that it lacked access to cosmopolitan sophistication; that notion is just a self-flattering label that status-conscious urbanites give to their own provincialisms. This young man's world was narrow in that it offered him only options for life defined within the enduring regime of power and deference that had been the baseline of everyday Delta life for more than a hundred years.

To be sure, things have changed, and in ways meaningful for those who live there. The local economy has diversified. Tallulah, a few miles away, is now a regional health care center, which offers employment less degraded than picking cotton. The area also bet heavily on prison construction and operation as a source of employment; on a subsequent trip I counted three penal facilities, one of which later gained national visibility as a shocking illustration of the scandal of privately-operated youth prisons and was closed as a result. Blacks also hold most elective offices in the area, and opportunities for decent employment and life with a modicum of dignity have increased substantially. Jim Crow is gone from public accommodations and routine commercial activity, and blacks and whites confront each other on equal terms as co-workers and consumers.

Yet, it is also apparent, especially to those familiar with the old order, that all these improvements have evolved from a foundation of social relations and class power built around the architecture of white supremacy. Vestiges of that foundation remain visible within current arrangements, and it can seem commonsensical, therefore, to suspect that it continues to shape the limits of the new structures of routine life. That is one reason, for example, that discussions of the relation between race and life chances in the contemporary United States gravitate so easily toward allusion to the explicit racial hierarchies that defined the Jim Crow era as an alternative to deep examination of the discrete processes that ground and reproduce inequality in the present. But commonsense rests on projection of the familiar and thereby stresses continuity over change. Unquestioned power and deference persist in the region, but their connection to race is no longer straightforward or easily predictable. The tendency to mistake superficially familiar imagery for actual continuity threatens to obscure how the present differs most meaningfully from the past.

On that 1993 trip, we left Transylvania and continued on to Eudora, where we visited with our remaining family there. Touré's first visit to Eudora in 1987 had a major impact on his perspective regarding class and gender in the early twentieth century. Our great-aunt, Ruth Bethune, was still alive then, and he learned from my father that she had graduated from Spelman College in 1915, I believe, and returned to her land-owning family in Eudora. Because there were no class-appropriate potential spouses for her, she spent the remainder of her life tending to and then caring for her parents and two brothers—Clarence, the mortician, and Jimmy, who had relocated for some years to Jackson, Mississippi, where he'd passed for white and then returned with one leg fewer than he'd had when he left and with no explanation for how he'd lost it. Her parents and both brothers had died many years before she did, and she lived out her days in the family home, eventually being cared for by younger relatives. As a not-quite seventeen-year-old, Touré was deeply moved to learn how her life and options seemed to have been constrained by the combination of class and gender ideology.

On the 1993 trip, we drove next to Little Rock accompanied by my father, retracing the remainder of the Delta region portion of the old Pine Bluff–New Orleans journey. Along the way, my father pointed out, as he often did on US 65, a point near Dumas where, for at least a century, one planter family owned all the land on either side of the highway, as far as the eye can see on the flat, sparse terrain for eight minutes while driving at sixty miles per hour.

A bit later we passed the Cummins State Prison. Cummins never had the wide reputation of its neighboring institutions, Parchman in Mississippi and Angola in Louisiana, but that was only because more of the famous bluesmen who memorialized savage southern prison farms came from those other states. In fact, Bill Clinton first entered the national spotlight, as a thirty-two-year-old governor, in relation to disclosure of the horrific discovery of corpses of prisoners who had been worked, beaten, or otherwise ill-treated to death at Cummins and buried over the years in unmarked graves without record or notification to loved ones. That day in 1993, through the vaporous heat rising from the dusty soil, we could see off in the distance phalanxes of prisoners in their white uniforms lining up and working, overseen by mounted guards with shotguns— exactly as they would have appeared four decades earlier.

In the late 1990s, on a visit to New Orleans, I stood at the takeout counter of Ye Olde College Inn, a restaurant on Carrollton Avenue in the Uptown section of the city, waiting for an order of oyster po-boy sandwiches—lightly breaded fried oysters on hard French bread and "dressed" with shredded lettuce, tomato, dill pickle slices and mayonnaise. I didn't go there often as a first option, though it was convenient from my mother's house. But the seafood po-boys were good, and my mother especially liked their oyster sandwich. My favorite purveyor of this local delicacy, Mulè's, had been badly damaged in a fire and had been tragically out of commission for more than two years.

Mulè's is in a black section of the Seventh Ward, and I'd frequented it since I was a kid. It was a place where men from the neighborhood would take their families for a meal of red beans and rice on the weekend or sit at the bar with cronies and convivially drink up a chunk of their week's wages. The restaurant had been black-owned for about twenty years, but its original proprietor was, or was believed to be, an Italian American who befriended and, the story goes, helped bankroll Fats Domino in his early years and managed his earnings, though some say possibly as much to Mulè's enrichment as to Fats's. After Fats became a national star, whenever he was in town, he'd leave his trademark baby pink and baby blue Cadillac parked outside, whether he was inside or not. All his past and current hits were on the jukebox. Mulè's served what still seems to me to be the best hot sausage po-boy in the city.

Whenever I entered Ye Olde College Inn, images of the restaurant under the segregationist regime tugged at the corners of my consciousness. We couldn't enter the dining room or even the separate bar entrance. What became after desegregation the general takeout counter was then the Jim Crow window, where we had to order and purchase our food. I never walked through the restaurant's front doors until the late 1970s.

As I stood there that day during Bill Clinton's presidency, a white man about my age came in to place and wait for his own order. We began chatting casually, as waiting customers do to pass the time. When it became clear that we shared the reservoir of an age cohort's memories, the conversation grew more amiable. We bonded around recollections of this and that, about music, school days, youth, sports, what used to be located where in the city. It was all pleasant enough, an enjoyable way to shorten the wait.

Then he drew the sum line that naturally follows from these middle-aged excursions into the nostalgic sweetness of lost youth. He remarked that those years, the period of our shared adolescence, had been a more desirable, more stable time than our middle-aged present. He gave no hint of lamenting the passage of the segregation era or its racial politics. Nor did he seem to be bemoaning the present in a racialized way, not even the indirect, coded, or blind ways that lurk within complaints about crime, family values, and so forth. Rather, his passing lament seemed purely actuarial, the generic stuff of coming to terms with aging. It's tempting to say that a black person wouldn't have been able to remember those years with the same oblivious fondness, but I know better. It was much easier for white people to live without noticing the segregationist architecture around which we all built our lives, and it is therefore easier for them to forget it in their recollections of the past. However, I've had too many similar conversations with nostalgic black baby boomers. Yet I certainly couldn't share that moment with him, least of all standing there at the takeout counter.

I very nearly said, "Well, though, thirty years ago we couldn't be here together to have this pleasant conversation, and I would have been prohibited by law from setting foot inside the dining room." But I didn't. I'm still not sure why I didn't; I had to swallow the words that were already in my mouth. I didn't respond with word or gesture. Maybe I didn't want to embarrass him; he seemed like a decent guy partaking of a casual conversation with another guy his age. Maybe I just didn't feel like enduring the seconds of awkward silence a comment would have caused or the longer, potentially more serious and stressful exchange that might have ensued. I well may have missed an opportunity for a useful bit of civic education or consciousness-raising. And I feel a little guilty and irresponsible when I consider that possibility. As it was, I just wanted to get my oyster sandwiches and go home.

Over the years, I've come to understand the deepest truth about the South of my youthful experience: it was a very particular moment in the history of the segregationist regime. Although this could be known only after the fact, after the reality had been made, the South within which I came of age—during the two decades after World War II—was the period when the white supremacist social order was coming apart at the seams. I have often pointed out to students that the Jim Crow order had a specific and relatively brief life span. It was not completely consolidated until the end of the first decade of the twentieth century. All of my grandparents were fully sentient and aware of their social environments, if not full adults, before the order's features took definite shape and assumed the form of normal politics and everyday life. And during the roughly three decades or so between the regime's consolidation and its slow, painful unraveling, the system was placed under considerable strain and reorganized internally by the Great Migration of black people out of the South or to cities within it, the Great Depression and the New Deal, the emergence of the industrial unions of the Congress of Industrial Organizations (CIO) and the war. And in large and small ways, black people never stopped challenging its boundaries and constraints—from the struggle over its imposition to its eventual defeat.

From that perspective, the segregationist order was never stable. It was only the white southern myth of timeless tradition, a myth installed partly at gunpoint as an element of consolidation of ruling class power, that gave it the appearance of solidity. Retracing that history, which contained and shaped but generally lies beyond the insight that can be drawn from personal experience, is necessary to fill in the picture of what the Jim Crow South was. However, because of the ways the past lives imagistically so near the surface of the present in the South, moments occasionally erupt that encourage, perhaps demand, critical reflection on the region's actual history and that history's relation to social and political life today.

The spring of 2017 produced such a moment in New Orleans. Two years earlier, Mayor Mitch Landrieu proposed removal of the city's four most conspicuous monuments to the Confederate insurrection on public display. Mayor Landrieu, the first white mayor since his father left office in 1978 and the first mayor to have received majorities of both blacks' and whites' votes since before the 1965 Voting Rights Act, proposed removing the monuments not long after then South Carolina Governor Nikki Haley announced the removal of the Confederate battle flag from the statehouse grounds in Columbia. The flag had flown at the statehouse since 1961, when it was placed atop the capitol as a gesture of defiant commitment to segregation in the face of civil rights activism; in a 2000 legislative compromise it was relocated to another spot on the grounds, near a statue of the state's legendary white supremacist terrorist, former governor and senator Benjamin "Pitchfork Ben" Tillman. Haley acted in the wake of Dylann Roof's race-inspired spree killing in a black church in Charleston and peremptorily ended a long-running controversy over the flag. Following her example, Mayor Landrieu proposed an ordinance mandating removal of four publicly displayed monuments, which the City Council passed in December 2015, with a 6-1 vote, the one dissent coming from a post-Katrina white politician who had built her career largely on catering to Uptown, upper-status whites by demonstrating her combativeness toward perceived black interests.

After more than a year of public discussion and debate, the first and most openly noxious of the four New Orleans monuments, the so-called Liberty Monument, finally was removed in April 2017. The monument was erected in 1891 to commemorate the explicitly white supremacist Crescent City White League's uprising perpetrated seventeen years earlier. The White League, which included many of the most prominent nominally white New Orleanians, including future Chief Justice of the US Supreme Court Edward Douglass White, represented itself as defenders of a "hereditary civilization and Christianity menaced by a stupid Africanization." It's worth noting that for decades many Italian Americans also were affronted by the monument, which they associated with the 1891 lynching of Sicilians by White League veterans who invoked the spirit of September 14, the date of the original insurrection, in their bloodlust. (In 2019, Mayor LaToya Cantrell, who is black and the city's first female to hold that office, issued an official apology for the lynching.) In 1932 the city added inscriptions to the obelisk that lauded the insurrection for having installed a government elected "by the white people" and praised the 1876 election that "recognized white supremacy in the South and gave us our state."

For nearly a century that monument was located at the foot of Canal Street, the city's symbolic entry point from the port. From the 1940s to the 1980s it was, after the Algiers ferry landing and a truly seedy tattoo parlor, the first thing one saw on entering the city. Its removal had been the source of earlier controversies in the mid-1970s and early 1990s, when it was eventually relocated from its prominent position and secluded between railroad tracks and power lines behind a hotel and the aquarium. The other monuments targeted for removal were a statue of Jefferson Davis, former president of the so-called Confederate States of America, erected in 1911; one of Robert E. Lee, commander of the insurrectionist army, erected in 1884; and one of P. G. T. Beauregard, another Confederate general, albeit one with ties to New Orleans, erected in 1915. I happened to be in New Orleans for the removal of the last three.

On May 1, I made a spur of the moment trip there, triggered by a message from a family member who hadn't been able to reach my mother for their regular early morning phone call. I'd gone up to New York a few days earlier to visit my dear friend, Judith Stein, who had just gone into hospice. I'd gotten worried calls like that before, but they were always false alarms. So until then my practice had been to wait a while and try to catch up with my mother later. That time, though, I immediately booked a flight. My mother was a few months from her ninety-fifth birthday and seemed to have slowed a bit on my visit a few weeks earlier. When I arrived on May Day, I noticed that she'd not performed some of her early morning rituals: the front gate was still locked; the newspapers were still in the front yard, and she hadn't opened the hurricane shutters on the front porch, all of which usually had been taken care of by dawn. We spent three good, quiet days together, and she seemed to rally on the third evening. But she woke up the following morning in considerable physical distress and died in the hospital that afternoon with many loving nieces and nephews near.

My mother had lived on her own and self-sufficiently for more than the last forty years of her life. Until a few weeks before her death she did laundry every day and cooked three meals a day. Her mind was sharp to the very end. For a number of years she'd carried a cane more as a fashion accessory than to help her walk. She relented only within the last decade to accept having a housecleaning service come once a month or so and only the night before she died consented to have someone come for a couple of hours in the morning to help her get the day started. (Her house is a couple of blocks away from the Fair Grounds, where the Jazz and Heritage Festival goes on every year during the last weekend of April and the first weekend of May. The crowds were a real peeve for her, particularly as festivalgoers often tried to block her driveway. The day she died was the beginning of the second weekend, and one of the cousins joked fondly in the hospital that she determined that she just couldn't bear another weekend of the commotion.) She was the oldest of my grandparents' four children and the last to die. Only one member of that generation remains in the extended family, my uncle and father of six of my first cousins. I'm the oldest of the next generation of a dozen and now oldest in our branch of the Macdonald bloodline in the United States.

I remained in the city for nearly a month after my mother's death and flew back to Philadelphia then mainly to rescue my car from a daily airport parking garage. I left assuming it was probably another false alarm and booked my return on May 4, thinking I could get in and out of the city between the two weekends of Jazz Fest. May turned out to be a particularly morbid month. Judith Stein died four days after my mother, and on Memorial Day I got word that an old, dear friend, more like a brother, from the GI anti-war movement had just entered hospice care in New Hampshire. I was able to get up there to see him. He died a little more than three months later, on my mother's birthday, the second dear friend and comrade to die on that date, though fifteen years apart.

Therefore, I was in New Orleans for nearly all the final, overheated controversy over removal of the monuments. The Liberty Monument was taken down with relatively little hubbub a week before I arrived in the city. Its odious history was so obvious that most of the monuments' defenders seemed prepared to concede that one. Not so for the other three. Each of them was "guarded" by ragtag bands of self-styled defenders of "heritage." They were by and large a motley crew, largely from out of town and outside the state. The group at the Beauregard monument, a couple of blocks from our house and which I passed for years on my daily walk through City Park, was anchored by a small squad who were living in the park out of a camper on the back of a pickup truck that advertised a Florida pet grooming business with a license plate reading PET KARE. A bumper sticker under the Confederate battle flag decal in a camper window sported the familiar canard "Heritage not Hate." The group's apparent leader, or at least its Energizer Bunny, was a hardscrabble woman whose generally animated performance suggested either crack or meth enthusiasm. She frequently marched around the statue waving the Bonnie Blue original flag of the Confederacy, wearing a bush hat, halter top, athletic shorts, and sneakers, with what looked like a pistol butt protruding from the top of her shorts. The group's posters linked "heritage art," praise for veterans, and, incongruously, love of Israel. One read, "First Davis, Then Jesus;" another proclaimed, "Wake Up Amerika, Marxism Is Here," and one protester tellingly sported a banner reading, "PRESIDENT TRUMP, MAKE AMERICA GREAT AGAIN." As I passed them one day, I overheard a woman waving a Don't Tread On Me flag mention to a fellow protester that she had to get something from her pastor.

The Jefferson Davis monument drew larger crowds of defenders, more heavily armed and boisterous, but also largely from out of town and including a man-bites-dog smattering of nonwhites, among them a young black man wearing a hoodie that covered his face in the heat of the day. Supporters of removing the monuments usually at least doubled the number of opponents. For all their posturing and enacting professional-wrestling-cum-*Red Dawn* cosplay fantasies, they melted away from the police presence at the moment of removal on May 11, the day after my mother's funeral. Some of them moved over to reinforce the crew at the Beauregard statue. The Lee statue was atop a ninety-foot pedestal at what was formerly Tivoli Circle or Place du Tivoli, a key node in the city, renamed Lee Circle, and which will be renamed again. It was also a site of clashes between largely out-of-towner "heritage" protesters and their opponents.

As I wrote on my mother's front porch six days after her funeral, the Beauregard statue—which was erected seven years before she was born—was being taken down. I could hear the sounds attending its removal, from both the machinery involved in the process and the competing chants of pro- and anti-monument protesters, which culminated in a loud cheer when it was taken away. The Lee statue was taken down two and a half days later. That ended the controversy, except for the occasional hiccup from disgruntled monument defenders, and the city finally is rid of those public celebrations of slavery and white supremacy that I'm hardly alone in having detested all my life.

I got involved in a neighborhood group chat discussion of the issue that began with complaints that taking down the Davis monument, which was on a busy thoroughfare, interfered with some commuters' route to work. As was to be expected, that complaint was quickly revealed as sanitizing garnish on the real objection, which was that the city should not have removed any of the monuments. Soon enough, the back and forth descended into all the predictable canards from the "heritage" crowd. (During the early 1990s fight over the Liberty Monument, historic preservationists and literal Klansmen— including David Duke—formed a tight bloc, often hiding behind bogus assertions of the quite ordinary monument's architectural significance.) Defenders resorted to sophistries and dizzyingly self-contradictory turns away from historical facts to feelings and a reactionary multiculturalism:

> The monuments are part of our history and therefore shouldn't be tampered with;
> They don't commemorate slavery or racism, just an abstract southern heritage;
> The Civil War wasn't about slavery but about states' rights and an abstract "way of life;"
> Removing the monuments only stirs up animosities, and we should let bygones be bygones;
> Blacks celebrate their history; whites should be able to celebrate theirs;

No one really cares about the monuments except opportun-
istic politicians;

Older black New Orleanians don't care about the monuments; only young militants and agitators do;

Only older blacks scarred by racism in the past care about
the monuments; younger blacks want to put the past
behind us and live as equals, not to keep fighting long-
dead slaveholders;

The monuments have aesthetic significance as distinct rep-
resentations of the architectural styles of their period;

Removing them is a diversion of public resources that would
be better devoted to addressing more pressing municipal
problems.

What was so striking about that discussion, as has been the
case with all others like it I've read or participated in, was the
absolute and intransigent refusal of defenders of Confederate
commemoration to confront brute, unambiguous historical
facts, beginning with the reasons for the treasonous rebellion. It's almost Freudian that many Confederate denialists
refer to the criminal insurrection as the "War of Northern
Aggression," although it was secessionists who rose in arms
against the United States government and Confederate troops
who initiated hostilities at Ft. Sumter. Beyond that, the most
preposterous denial—either clinical, dishonest, ignorant, or
some combination of the three—is the claim that the insurrection had any motivation apart from defense of slavery.
Alexander Stephens, former Whig congressman from Georgia
and Vice-President of the Confederacy, made clear in his
famous 1861 "Cornerstone Speech" that

the new [i.e., Confederate] constitution has put at rest, forever, all the agitating questions relating to our peculiar institution— African slavery as it exists among us—the proper status of the negro in our form of civilization. This was the immediate cause of the late rupture and present revolution.

Stephens went on to say:

Our new government is founded upon exactly the opposite idea [from the Founders' presumption that all men are equal]; its foundations are laid, its cornerstone rests, upon the great truth that the negro is not equal to the white man; that slavery—subordination to the superior race—is his natural and normal condition. This, our new government, is the first, in the history of the world, based upon this great physical, philosophical, and moral truth.[2]

South Carolina's "Declaration of the Immediate Causes Which Induce and Justify the Secession of South Carolina from the Federal Union" of 1860 made clear:

Those [non-slaveholding] states have assumed the right of deciding upon the propriety of our domestic institutions; and have denied the rights of property established in fifteen of the states and recognized by the Constitution; they have denounced as sinful the institution of slavery; they have permitted open establishment among them of societies, whose avowed object is to disturb the peace and to eloign the property of the citizens of other states. They have encouraged and assisted thousands of our slaves to leave their homes; and those who remain, have been incited by emissaries, books and

pictures to servile insurrection. For twenty-five years this agitation has been steadily increasing, until it has now secured to
its aid the power of the common Government. Observing the
forms of the Constitution, a sectional party has found within
that Article establishing the Executive Department, the means
of subverting the Constitution itself. A geographical line has
been drawn across the Union, and all the States north of that
line have united in the election of a man to the high office of
President of the United States, whose opinions and purposes
are hostile to slavery. He is to be entrusted with the administration of the common Government, because he has declared
that that "Government cannot endure permanently half slave,
half free," and that the public mind must rest in the belief
that slavery is in the course of ultimate extinction. This sectional combination for the subversion of the Constitution has
been aided, in some of the States, by elevating to citizenship,
persons who, by the supreme law of the land are incapable of
becoming citizens; and their votes have been used to inaugu-
rate a new policy, hostile to the South, and destructive of its
beliefs and safety. On the 4th day of March next, this party will
take possession of the Government. It has announced that the
South shall be excluded from the common territory [that is,
the territories acquired from Mexico in 1848], that the judicial
tribunals shall be made sectional, and that a war must be waged
against slavery until it shall cease throughout the United States.
The guarantees of the Constitution will then no longer exist;
the equal rights of the States will be lost. The slaveholding
States will no longer have the power of self-government, or
self-protection, and the Federal Government will have become
their enemy.[3]

Each rebellious state's Ordinance of Secession made clear that the key characteristic uniting their confederation was commitment to slavery; all referred to their collectivity as "the slaveholding states." Most declared explicitly that the immediate precipitant for their action was Abraham Lincoln's election to the presidency, which they took as a provocation because of his and the Republicans' open opposition to slavery. And they were correct to feel provoked.

As historian James Oakes argues brilliantly in *The Scorpion's Sting: Antislavery and the Coming of the Civil War*, Lincoln and other Republicans embraced a tradition of antislavery constitutionalism that reached back decades.[4] That view held that the United States was founded on the principle that all men are free, based on the Law of Nations and affirmed by the 1772 British *Somerset* case. Adherents to antislavery constitutionalism accepted slavery as protected by the Constitution where it existed at the Founding. However, they insisted that its further expansion was not only not constitutionally protected but would violate the fundamental principle of universal freedom and thus the Constitution. They hoped (naïvely, it would turn out) that the border states, where plantation production was relatively minor—Delaware, Maryland, Kentucky, and Missouri—could be induced by the superiority of free labor to abolish slavery on their own. Their strategy for abolition was to restrict the institution to the plantation states, where, the theory went, it would wither and die (thus the common metaphor at the time of the cornered scorpion that stings itself to death). That strategy is what underlay the South Carolina Declaration's assertion that Lincoln desired to put slavery "in the course of ultimate extinction." From the antislavery constitutionalist standpoint, the only basis for direct federal interference with slavery in the states where the institution was protected was "military emancipation," which Republicans repeatedly threatened to use to suppress a proslavery rebellion. Ironically, secessionists provided the opportunity to do just that.

To return to the 2017 monuments controversy, some advocates of leaving the statues in place contended that each of the three men commemorated is politically and historically significant for reasons other than fighting to preserve slavery. In response to a suggestion that the monuments could remain if accompanied by curatorial statements that indicate the unsanitized truth about the insurrection and its objectives, which are repugnant to values of equality, justice, and democracy, one contributor to the neighborhood group chat discussion proposed that plaques should acknowledge "the roles of the Generals and President BEFORE, DURING, and AFTER as significant as the DURING," as though running an insurance company, holding office in antebellum congresses, owning plantations, being a career soldier, college president, or railroad executive were equivalent to rising in treasonous insurrection for the sole purpose of protecting slavery and thus throwing the nation into its deadliest war. (And, yes, Lee may—or may not, the story is likely apocryphal—have expelled some white students for assaulting blacks, after he lost the war to keep them enslaved.) Yet each statue identifies its subject only with the Confederate insurrection, and Beauregard and Lee are depicted in their military uniforms. And that is as it should be because that is their sole distinctive place in history. Can we imagine a statue honoring Hermann Göring for his exploits as a World War I aviator?

The reality is that the monuments' deeper historical significance is not that they celebrate the Confederacy. It's more meaningful that they were erected between 1884 and 1915, the precise period when the city's governing elites disfranchised blacks and imposed a violent white supremacist social and political order, including the Jim Crow regime. That timing is significant because it coincides with the construction and propagation of Lost Cause ideology across the region in concert with the program of restoration of unmitigated upper-class dominance in the South after the defeat of Reconstruction and the Populist movement.

Mass disfranchisement, not only of nearly all blacks— more than 104,000 black people voted in Louisiana in the 1896 election; fewer than 1,000 voted in 1904, and fewer than 400 in a total black population of more than 100,000 were registered to vote in New Orleans as late as 1940—but also many poor whites, was a key element of that program, along with imposition of the apartheid regime. Blacks were clearly the principal targets of the juggernaut, but removing them from political life also deprived working-class whites of potential allies for challenging ruling-class prerogatives. Erection of those monuments was an element in consolidation of that order. The monuments were intended to memorialize the myth of a distinctive (white) southern identity and tradition then being invented and imposed by force and made common sense "truth" through unchallenged repetition.

When I was a teen during the last years of codified segregation, there were some neighborhoods in the city I carefully avoided and felt uncomfortable in—if not actively fearful— when I couldn't avoid them. I still don't know my way around them very well. Only decades later, on reading Thomas Hanchett's *Sorting Out the New South City: Race, Class, and Urban Development in Charlotte, 1875–1975*, which shows that neighborhood segregation in Charlotte, North Carolina was a twentieth-century phenomenon, did it crystallize in my head that all those neighborhoods that raised the hair on my neck were post–World War I developments.[5] As in other southern cities, older neighborhoods, like my family's, were often mixed in one form or another—alternating blocks, opposite sides of the street, sections of blocks. Systematic residential segregation, that is, wasn't part of an organic "way of life." It was a product of the confluence of nascent city planning and the growth of a residential real estate market that invented the idea of the neighborhood, homogeneous by race and class, as an ideal statement of one's place in the social order. In the urban South those processes of residential segmentation played out within the framework of consolidating class power under the rubric of white supremacy and strict racial separation. That's why the most rigidly segregated neighborhoods were among those developed between the early twentieth century and the early 1960s.

Lost Cause ideology and the mythology of the Solid South were cudgels employed to demand political conformity among whites and to stifle dissent from ruling-class agendas as well as to suppress blacks. In his definitive study of disfranchisement, *The Shaping of Southern Politics: Suffrage Restriction and the Establishment of the One-Party South, 1880–1910*, J. Morgan Kousser quotes North Carolina Governor Charles B. Aycock, who made the point succinctly, writing several years after a violent 1898 Democratic putsch ousted the interracial Populist-Republican-Fusion government that had won consecutive statewide elections: "The Democratic party is alone sufficient. We need a united people. We need the combined effort of every North Carolinian. We need the strength which comes from believing alike."[6] Segregation was enforced on whites as well as blacks.

That reality is obscured in a contemporary perspective that flattens out history and context into a simple polarity of racism/anti-racism and reduces politics to an unchanging contest of black and white. That perspective compresses historical distinctions between slavery and Jim Crow and ignores the generation of struggle, often enough biracial or interracial, against ruling class power over defining the political and economic character of the post-Emancipation South, as well as ongoing struggle against and within the new order as it consolidated. In 1892, the same year Homer A. Plessy challenged the state's new Separate Car Act, black and white workers in New Orleans conducted a largely successful general strike in the face of the opposition's attempt to incite racial division among the strikers. In *Waterfront Workers of New Orleans: Race, Class, and Politics, 1863–1923*, Eric Arnesen documents a complex history of interracial and biracial solidarity and tensions among the city's strong dock unions even during the high period of ruling class revanchism and codification of segregation.[7] And New Orleans was hardly unique in that regard.

Such popular support as there is among whites today for Confederate nostalgia is in part the product of that regime's success and its ideological dominance for a century or more. Lost Cause ideology was propagated aggressively, nationally as well as regionally, as part of southern elites' crusade advocating "sectional reconciliation" on white supremacist terms that would undermine enforcement of black southerners' constitutional rights and give the southern ruling class a free hand in establishing and maintaining its new order. It was a cornerstone of the "New South" program associated with Atlanta journalist Henry Grady and others, and it was propounded as historical fact by prominent intellectuals like Columbia University historian William A. Dunning and Woodrow Wilson—Princeton historian, political scientist and president, New Jersey governor, and eventual US president. It was projected through popular culture in films like D. W. Griffith's 1915 *Birth of a Nation* and its 1939 talkie update, *Gone with the Wind,* which has been perhaps more influential than any other cultural product in disseminating and perpetuating the Lost Cause fantasy.

There is an additional layer of complexity surrounding the monuments controversy that also speaks to the region's distinctive brew of continuity and change. Just as the monuments were erected in service to specific historical objectives, the campaign for their removal memorializes its time and context and affirms the current social and cultural order. Repudiation of Confederate mythology and Lost Cause ideology, perhaps especially because it is so long overdue, celebrates the current regime of class and social power. Mayor Landrieu's eloquent and heartfelt address hours before the last monument was taken down, while even quoting Stephens's "Cornerstone Speech" to drive home what the statues actually commemorated, drew an instructive contrast between then and now:

> The historic record is clear: the Robert E. Lee, Jefferson Davis, and P. G. T. Beauregard statues were not erected just to honor these men, but as part of the movement which became known as The Cult of the Lost Cause. This "cult" had one goal— through monuments and through other means—to rewrite history to hide the truth, which is that the Confederacy was on the wrong side of humanity ...

This is, however, about showing the whole world that we as a city and as a people are able to acknowledge, understand, reconcile and, most importantly, choose a better future for ourselves, making straight what has been crooked and making right what was wrong.[8]

At the same time that the Mayor and City Council acted courageously and progressively in ridding the city of those monuments to a loathsome past, the new regime that removal celebrates, as some skeptics note, rests on commitments to policies that intensify economic inequality on a scale that makes New Orleans one of the most unequal cities in the United States. The processes driving this regime had been evolving since the early 1970s and the administration of Mayor Landrieu's father, Moon, who is, like his son, a sincere civil rights egalitarian. (Moon also has been my uncle's close friend since they were in law school together in the 1950s, during Loyola University's early years of desegregation.) Local government contributes to this deepening inequality through such means as cuts to the public sector, privatization of public goods and services, and support of upward redistribution through shifting public resources from service provision to subsidy for private, rent-intensifying redevelopment (commonly but too ambiguously called "gentrification"). These processes, often summarized as neoliberalization, do not target blacks as blacks, and, as in other cities, coincided with emergence of black public officialdom in and after the elder Landrieu's mayoralty and continued unabated through the thirty-two years of black-led local government between the two Landrieus and into the black-led administration that succeeded Mitch.

Both the processes of neoliberalization and racial integration of the city's governing elite accelerated in the aftermath of Hurricane Katrina. It may seem ironic because of how the visual imagery of dispossession and displacement after Katrina came universally to signify the persistence of racial injustice, but a generally unrecognized feature of the post-Katrina political landscape is that the city's governing class is now more seamlessly interracial than ever. That is, or should be, an unsurprising outcome four decades after racial transition in local government and the emergence and consolidation of a strong black political and business class, increasingly well incorporated into the structures of governing. It has been encouraged as well by the city's commitment to cultural and heritage tourism, which, as comes through in Mayor Landrieu's remarks on the monuments, is anchored to a discourse of multiculturalism and diversity. And generational succession has brought to prominence cohorts among black and white elites who increasingly have attended the same schools; lived in the same neighborhoods; participated in the same voluntary associations; and share cultural and consumer tastes, worldviews, and political and economic priorities.

Neighborhoods that are nearly homogeneously white remain, for example, but on closer examination class defines their exclusivity at least as much as race. My automatic reflex to flinch in them is more a reflection of vestiges of the past than of current realities. A nonwhite person may still draw unwanted attention in such neighborhoods, but it is now more likely because race is a visible shorthand for class. And that shorthand can lead to instances of mistaken identity in which racial cues might overwhelm class cues; in such instances myopically vigilant, or bigoted, neighbors might look askance at possible interlopers, at extremes even challenge them or call the police. It's not unthinkable that such encounters might at the extremes become unpleasant or even dangerous. Yet the difference between then and now is the difference between normal and extreme; it is also the difference between having recourse to legal protection and not. Failure to recognize the importance of those differences is what makes possible claims that nothing has changed; it is also why those claims are counterproductive for both historical understanding and political strategy.

Signs that the city's governing class was becoming more integrated racially were visible even before Katrina. That's why pundits' and academics' doomsday predictions that Mitch Landrieu's election in 2010, along with a white Council majority, augured the displacement of black political power and a return to the Jim Crow status quo ante were naïve. (Hysterical reaction was exacerbated by the circumstance that a serious, though ultimately unsuccessful, white candidate was challenging for Atlanta's mayoralty around the same time.) Despite some whites' random fantasies of "taking back the city" and developers' enthusiasm for what they perceived as an opportunity, a "clean slate," to remake it as an upscale theme park, the de facto ruling class made clear that it had no desire to break decisively from the interracial or biracial regime that had governed the city for decades. The 2014 election, in which Landrieu was reelected, again with majorities of blacks' and whites' votes, also reversed the 5-2 white majority on the City Council, which has two at-large posts, elected citywide, and five elected from Districts, apportioned into two solidly black districts, one solidly white, and two that are racially competitive. The 2017 election, which brought Mayor Cantrell to power as the first woman to hold the office, along with three female councilmembers, produced a council with three black members, two whites, one Mexican American, and a Vietnamese American. (The latter defeated the black incumbent in the demographically blackest district, which also has a significant Vietnamese American population.) The two at-large posts were won by a black man and the Mexican American woman, who previously held a state legislative seat from a predominantly black district.

Misplaced anxieties about the significance of the 2010 election exposed another way that fantasies about the southern past live within and distort perspectives on the present. It's hardly fanciful to assume that some element among ruling class whites still find black-led government distasteful, and, as the monument controversy underscored, no shortage of white New Orleanians harbor racist views, often embedded in the babble about "heritage." One of my cousins, who was then a municipal official, was accosted at a public event nearly two years after the monuments' removal by a hardcore opponent still smarting over it. After calmly parrying his stream of sophistries, all located on the list I note above, she politely extricated herself from the interaction. As she walked away, he called after her, "You should be grateful that you're here," one of the oldest and ugliest of slavery apologists' canards. Nevertheless, no matter how common such views may be, they do not define the dispositions of the white governing and opinion-shaping strata, who have made clear that, at a minimum, they see no apparent advantage in expending effort to displace the interracial regime, especially none that would outweigh the disruption and instability attempting to do so would create. After all, things have been working quite comfortably for white political and economic elites as well as for black ones.

Fear that loss of a black electoral majority would result in a return to the political and civic exclusion that defined the Jim Crow era betrays a fundamental misunderstanding of both past and present as well as how they relate. Despite what the monuments have symbolized, politics in New Orleans, or elsewhere in the South, cannot be reduced to an unbroken arc of racial subordination continuous from the segregation era, the Civil War, or slavery. That past, or more accurately those pasts, while testament to the brutality and horrors of earlier systems of exploitation, are not the deeper Truth of contemporary inequalities, not even necessarily those that may seem most conspicuously racial. Just as the Ku Klux Klan today has none of the social and political power that the earlier versions had in the 1960s, 1920s, or 1880s, neither can anything about those monuments shed light on the sources of contemporary inequality and injustice. Allegory might be rhetorically powerful, but it is not adequate as analysis or explanation. In this case it can also be a dodge to sidestep the mechanisms that actually reproduce inequality in the present.

As obnoxious as the monuments are, removing them was ultimately a rearguard undertaking and one entirely compatible with the dominant neoliberal ideal of social and racial justice as celebration of "rich multicultural heritage" and genuine upward mobility for individuals without regard to race, gender, sexual orientation, and so on within a social order that is sharply unequal for most. And for reasons that have less to do with an abstraction like white supremacy than with the dynamics of a political and economic regime that concentrates benefits at the top at the expense of everyone else, black New Orleanians are disproportionately—but by no means entirely or exclusively—likely to occupy the ranks of the dispossessed under that regime. And the terms on which the white supremacist past has been acknowledged and repudiated actually obscure the sources of inequality and dispossession today.

While the segregationist system was clearly and obviously racist and white supremacist, it wasn't merely about white supremacy for its own sake alone. It was the instrument of a specific order of political and economic power that was clearly racial but that most fundamentally stabilized and reinforced the dominance of powerful political and economic interests. White supremacy was and remains an ideology, and a very abstract one at that, and because it's so abstract—its basic premises and categories are fantasies—its practical warrants are always improvised. For example, white supremacy sometimes required physical segregation, sometimes did not, and efforts to impose the ideology as reality always were haunted by trade-offs between principle and practicality, including the ultimate impossibility of racial classification. White supremacy, that is, was as much a cover story as a concrete program, even though it was by far the most immediately visible and consequential aspect of the segregationist order.

New Orleans is unquestionably better for having been ridden of the monuments and public commemoration of both the mythology and the actual history they validate. The Mayor and City Council, as well as all New Orleanians who supported their removal, are to be commended for that accomplishment. Arguably, it would've been better if the victory were the product of a broader coalition and deeper public education, for example, with greater attention to the reality that Lost Cause ideology and Jim Crow were imposed on whites as well as blacks, but we seldom win such victories on ideal terms. Perhaps this controversy and its successful resolution could provide a template for helping to counter the dangerous right wing's ability to mobilize around that mythology to camouflage its deeper inegalitarian class program in the present. However, that potential is undercut by the fact that celebration of progress from a benighted racist past settles onto narrow, moralistic terms of having overcome racial exclusion and bigotry to realize inclusion and diversity.

This narrative has emerged as a signature of the newest, post-segregation era version of the New South. Cities and towns all over the region have altered their symbolic architecture and cultural expressions, material and otherwise, to reflect the new regime of racial inclusion and equality. Larger, or tourist destination, cities like New Orleans, Atlanta, Charleston, Birmingham, Charlotte, Richmond, or Memphis have marked the new racial order by erecting and removing (the latter often enough with controversy as in New Orleans) statuary and flags, changing street names, placing historical markers, supporting museums and the like. Civil rights tourism has become a multibillion-dollar niche within the historical/heritage tourism industry. In East Carroll Parish, Louisiana, which abuts Arkansas and Mississippi in the Mississippi Delta region, tiny Lake Providence is home to a Louisiana State Cotton Museum that presents a surprisingly unvarnished account of slavery and the sharecrop system. Across the river, practically every hamlet on US Highway 61 between Greenville, Mississippi and Memphis advertises a blues museum or black history memorial (or both).

Developments such as these do sharply punctuate the passage of the old regime, especially for those old enough to recall the Jim Crow era as everyday life. (Lake Providence, for instance, was one of the places we definitely did not want to stop on road trips when I was a kid.) As I've spent more time in the region in recent decades, I've gradually realized what gave me that eerie, out-of-time sense there. The Jim Crow racial order has been vanquished. That is clearest at the level that defines daily life and aspirations. Removal of the strictures of official apartheid has radically altered opportunity structures and patterns of work, quality of life, and social relations in small and large ways that aren't readily apparent to those who didn't know the old order. Working together as equals encourages socializing together, which is also enabled by elimination of the petty apartheid of Jim Crow in public accommodations. Occasionally, when I notice an interracial group of co-workers or friends out in a restaurant, bar, or the like, I recall how utterly impossible that would have been as late as 1960.

As the region has continued to evolve away from the Jim Crow era, I've also come to understand what felt like the unsettling continuity within the large fabric of change. In part, the sensation derived from the persistence of habituated conventions of interaction that evoke earlier racial etiquette, which superficially conjures images of the racial hierarchy that grounded that etiquette. But that imagery also is largely scar tissue from having lived under Jim Crow, of the same sort as that indicated in the fear that loss of a black-led government would usher in a return of the old order, or my musing that a conductor would instruct me to give up my business class seat to a white passenger. What seem to be vestiges of the Jim Crow world in a sense are just that. But passage of the old order's segregationist trappings throws into relief the deeper reality that what appeared and was experienced as racial hierarchy was also class hierarchy. Now blacks occupy positions in the socioeconomic order previously available only to whites, and whites occupy those previously identified with blacks. And the dynamics of superordination and subordination, patterns of appropriation and distribution, and dominant understandings of which material interests should drive policy remain much as they were.

This underscores the point that the core of the Jim Crow order was a class system rooted in employment and production relations that were imposed, stabilized, regulated, and naturalized through a regime of white supremacist law, practice, custom, rhetoric, and ideology. Defeating the white supremacist regime was a tremendous victory for social justice and egalitarian interests. At the same time, that victory left the undergirding class system untouched and in practical terms affirmed it. That is the source of that bizarre sensation I felt in the region a generation after the defeat of Jim Crow. The larger takeaway from this reality is that a simple racism/anti-racism framework isn't adequate for making sense of the segregation era, and it certainly isn't up to the task of interpreting what has succeeded it or challenging the forms of inequality and injustice that persist.

As I noted at the outset, I was prompted to undertake this rumination partly by the sense that my age cohort, those born in the first decade or so of the postwar baby boom, very soon will be the last living Americans with direct knowledge and recollections of the Jim Crow era. I felt, therefore, that it could be useful to leave some sort of account as a record. I make no claim to generality, much less universality. I'm very much aware that my perspective is very partial, shaped by where I lived and when, class position and family circumstances, and my age during those years. I've tried to keep those and other qualifications in mind and not to overclaim, as well as to be empathetic to other perspectives.

The feeling of the passing from the stage of history of an era and the people who lived it has been intensified by the coincidence of my mother's death and the removal of the odious New Orleans monuments to white supremacist rule. I know that before long my cohort will also be the only living Americans with active knowledge or recollections of "the Sixties." It's interesting to be in this position, but it happens to everyone who lives long enough. Nevertheless, it is bemusing to observe when formative periods of one's past become grist for scholarly, ideological, and casual interpretation and debate and are constructed and reconstructed from the standpoint of current concerns and debates. That's also inevitable, on one level what history is. A danger, however, is that, when reckoning with the past becomes too much like allegory, its nuances and contingencies, its essential open-endedness, can disappear. Then history can become either a narrative of inevitable, progressive unfolding to the present or, worse, a tendentious assertion that nothing has ever changed, and both divesting the past of its discrete foreignness and contingency or reducing it to the warm-up act for the present are handmaidens of ruling class power. The danger of that tendency is especially great in moments of ruling class triumphalism such as this one.

In such moments, longevity can be a source of corrective optimism. I recall an occasion early in the George W. Bush presidency when my friend and former physician, Quentin Young, was confronted at a talk by a medical student who lamented that she couldn't imagine being able to win any progressive objectives because the right had been in power all her conscious life. Quentin, who was then about eighty years old, responded that a virtue of having lived as long as he had was that he knew that almost no one, no matter how far left or how optimistic, standing in 1950 would have predicted that the back of the Jim Crow system would be broken within fifteen years. He was correct, and that's a good lesson for us all to keep in mind in this most perilous time in this country and the world.

Notes

Foreword

1 E. P. Thompson, *The Making of the English Working Class*, London: Vintage, 1966, 12.

2 Richard Wright, "The Ethics of Living Jim Crow," in *Uncle Tom's Children*, New York: Library of America, 1991, 237.

Introduction

1 Charles A. Lofgren, *The Plessy Case: A Legal-Historical Interpretation*, New York: Oxford University Press, 1987.

3. The New Order Taking Shape within the Old

1 Peter Novick, *The Holocaust in American Life*, Boston: Mariner Books, 2000.

2 Brewton Berry, *Almost White: A Study of Certain Racial Hybrids in the Eastern United States*, New York: Macmillan, 1963.

3 See, e.g., Adolph L. Reed Jr., "From Jenner to Dolezal: One Trans Good, the Other Not So Much," *Common Dreams*, June 15, 2015.

4 George Stocking, Jr., *Race, Culture, and Evolution: Essays in the History of Anthropology*, Chicago: University of Chicago Press, 1968, 265.

5 Melissa Fay Greene, *Praying for Sheetrock*, Boston: Da Capo Press, 2006.

4. The Obsolescence of "Passing"

1 St. Clair Drake and Horace Cayton Jr., *Black Metropolis: A Study of Negro Life in a Northern City*, Chicago: University of Chicago Press, 1945.
2 Letter from Walter A. Plecker, M.D., State Registrar of Vital Statistics to Local Registrars, Physicians, Health Officers, School Superintendents, and Clerks of the Courts, January 1943, in author's possession.
3 Ibid.
4 Horace Kallen, "Aspects of the Jewish Position in the Economic and Social Orders," *American Jewish Chronicle*, October 11, 1918, 551.

5. Echoes, Scar Tissue, and Historicity

1 John M. Barry, *Rising Tide: The Great Mississippi Flood of 1927 and How It Changed America*, New York: Touchstone Books, 1997.
2 Alexander Stephens, "The 'Cornerstone Speech,'" Savannah, Georgia, March 21, 1861 at battlefields.org.
3 South Carolina Convention, "Declaration of the Immediate Causes Which Induce and Justify the Secession of South Carolina from the Federal Union; and the Ordinance of Secession," Evans & Cogswell, printers to the Convention, 1860.
4 James Oakes, *The Scorpion's Sting: Antislavery and the Coming of the Civil War*, New York: W. W. Norton, 2015.
5 Thomas Hanchett, *Sorting Out the New South City: Race, Class, and Urban Development in Charlotte, 1875–1975*, Chapel Hill: University of North Carolina Press, 1998.
6 J. Morgan Kousser, *The Shaping of Southern Politics: Suffrage Restriction and the Establishment of the One-Party South, 1880–1910*, New Haven, CT: Yale University Press, 1974, 78.

7 Eric Arnesen, *Waterfront Workers of New Orleans: Race, Class, and Politics, 1863–1923*, Champaign: University of Illinois Press, 1994.

8 "Mitch Landrieu's Speech on the Removal of Confederate Monuments in New Orleans," *New York Times*, May 23, 2017.

Adolph L. Reed Jr. is professor emeritus of Political Science at the University of Pennsylvania. He taught previously at the New School for Social Research, the University of Illinois at Chicago, Northwestern, Yale, and Howard universities. He was a 2002/2003 Carnegie Corporation Scholar of Vision. In 2019 he was the inaugural McKenna scholar in residence at the Frank McKenna Centre for Leadership at St. Francis Xavier University and in 1998/99 was the John J. McCloy class of '16 professor at Amherst College. In 2013, he was Featured International Speaker, at the invitation of the minister of the Presidential Secretariat, at the national symposium in Brasilia marking the tenth anniversary of the Brazilian Presidential Secretariat for the Promotion of Racial Equality.

He is author and editor of seven other books, including the award-winning *W. E. B. Du Bois and American Political Thought* and *Class Notes,* a collection of his popular essays. He has been a regular columnist in the *Progressive, Village Voice,* and *New Republic.* He has published numerous articles in the *Nation, Harper's Magazine, Dissent, Common Dreams*, as well as nonsite.org, of which he serves on the editorial board, as well as a variety of other scholarly journals. He has served on the boards of Public Citizen, Food and Water Action, and the Debs-Jones-Douglass Institute. He has served on the executive council of the American Political Science Association, the executive committee and national council of the American Association of University Professors and the AAUP's Committee on Academic Freedom and Tenure, and was a member of the Interim National Council of the Labor Party.